Terminal Iron Works

Terminal Iron Works

The Sculpture of David Smith

Rosalind E. Krauss

The MIT Press Cambridge, Massachusetts, and London, England

Preface

My knowledge of modern painting and sculpture was developed largely through the critical essays of, and discussions with, Clement Greenberg and Michael Fried. With their aid I began, in the early sixties, to write criticism. It was during this period of intense study of modernist works of art that my own conviction about the quality of American sculpture was strengthened, and with it my desire to write about David Smith. I am deeply grateful to Clement Greenberg, who, not only as an executor of the Smith Estate but as a friend, helped the present work to come into being. I wish to thank him and the other executors, Robert Motherwell and Ira Lowe, for having given me access to the material in David Smith's archive and to the works and papers still at the studio in Bolton Landing, New York. On repeated trips to Bolton Landing, Smith's former assistant, Leon Pratt, patiently helped me to lift and carry hundreds of pounds of sculpture, page through countless drawings, and answer questions about Smith's working process. In Detroit, Garnett McCoy at the Archives of American Art discussed with me the experience that he, as a builder of the Smith Archive, had of the material. Where not otherwise indicated in the credits on p. xiv, all photographs of Smith's sculpture are by David Smith himself. I am grateful to the Archive and to the Estate for permission to use these photographs.

I am profoundly indebted to Dorothy Dehner and Jean Freas Smith for indulging my many interviews and answering questions about Smith's life and art for which I would have had no other source. I am indebted as well to all the collectors who provided me with information about the Smith works in their possession, especially to Lucille Corcos Levy, Edward Levy, and Mildred Constantine, who generously supplied me with details about Smith's life in the thirties.

There are no sufficient thanks for the help and encouragement Richard Krauss extended to me during the preparation of this work; this is therefore merely a public acknowledgment of that support.

23
Alberto Giacometti. *Woman with Her Throat Cut*. 1932. Bronze, 34½ inches. Museum of Modern Art, New York.
24
Reclining Construction. 1936. Iron, 14 × 26⅞ × 6⅛ inches. Estate of the artist.
25
Reclining Figure. 1953. Steel, 25½ × 13½ × 3½ inches. Estate of the artist.
26
Aftermath Figure. 1945. Bronze, 13⅜ × 7⅝ × 3 inches. Estate of the artist.
27
Oculus. 1947. Steel, 37 × 32½ × 10 inches. Collection Robert E. John, New York.
28
House in Landscape. 1945. Steel, 18½ × 24¾ × 6 inches. Collection George Irwin, Quincy, Illinois.
29
The Banquet. 1951. Steel, 53⅛ × 80¾ × 13½ inches. Private collection.
30
Tanktotem IV. 1953. Steel, 92½ × 33½ × 29 inches. Albright-Knox Gallery, Buffalo.
Tanktotem III. 1953. Steel, 84½ × 27 × 20 inches. Estate of the artist.
31
Tanktotem V. 1955–1956. Steel, 96¾ × 52 inches. Collection Howard and Jean Lipman, Cannondale, Connecticut.
32
Sentinel IV. 1957. Steel, painted black, 80 × 29 × 32 inches. Private collection.
33
Voltri XIII. 1962. Steel, 64⅛ × 103¾ inches. Estate of the artist.
34
Voltri, Italy. 1962.
35
Spoleto, Italy. 1962.
36
Zig IV. (side view)
37a
Zig VII. 1963. Steel, painted cream, red, and blue, 94¾ × 100⅜ inches. Estate of the artist.
37b
Zig VIII. 1964. Steel, painted red, black, and white, 100¾ × 87½ inches. Museum of Fine Arts, Boston.
38
Zig VII and *Zig VIII*. (alternate views)
39
War Landscape. 1947. Bronze, 9 × 7 × 6 inches. Estate of the artist.
40
Uncatalogued page in the Archive. Early 1940s.
41
Uncatalogued page in the Archive. Early 1940s.
42
Page from Sketchbook #41. 1944–1954. Archive IV/58.
43
Pieter Breughel. Detail from *Sloth*. 1557. One of a series of engravings of *The Seven Deadly Sins*.
44
Page from a 1945 sketchbook. Archive IV/51.
45
One of the two fields at Bolton Landing in which Smith set out his sculpture.
46
Untitled etching. 1942. Estate of the artist.
47
Untitled etching. 1942. Estate of the artist.

48
Page from Notebook #27. Mid-1940s. Archive III/997.

49
Atrocity. 1943. Bronze, 4 × 6½ × 3¼ inches. Collection Mr. and Mrs. Lester Talkington, Tappan, New York.

50
Page from Sketchbook #23. 1933–1945. Archive III/838.

51
The Rape. 1945. Bronze, 9 × 5⅜ × 3½ inches. Collection Mr. and Mrs. Stephen Paine, Boston.

52
Spectre Riding the Golden Ass. 1945. Bronze, 11¾ × 12¼ × 4 inches. Detroit Institute of Art.

53
Medal for Dishonor: Propaganda for War. 1939–1940. Bronze, 11⅜ × 9⅜ inches. Joseph H. Hirshhorn Collection, New York.

54
Page from Sketchbook #41. 1944–1954. Archive IV/32.

55
Untitled. 1955. Clay, 10 × 5¼ × 4½ inches. Estate of the artist.

56
36 Birdheads. 1950. Steel, blue aluminum paint, 55 × 36¼ inches. Collection Mr. and Mrs. Lee N. Baker, Baltimore.

57
Tanktotem I. 1952. Steel, 90 × 39 inches. Art Institute of Chicago.

58
Daumier. *My Velocipede!* Lithograph published in *Charivari*, September 17, 1868. Tacked on a window mullion in Smith's living room at Bolton Landing.

59
Woman in a Room. 1945. Bronze, 12 × 9¼ inches. Estate of the artist.

60
Hudson River Landscape. 1951. Steel and stainless steel, 49½ × 75 × 16¼ inches. Whitney Museum of American Art, New York.

61
Tanktotem VII. 1960. Steel, painted blue, dark blue, and white, 84½ × 36¾ × 14⅛ inches. Storm King Art Center, Mountainville, New York.

62
Voltri-Bolton V. 1962. Steel, drybrushed with orange paint, 86½ × 34 × 24 inches. Collection Mr. and Mrs. John Braston, San Francisco.

63
Helmholtzian Landscape. 1946. Painted steel, 15⅞ × 17⅝ × 7⅛ inches. Collection David Lloyd Kreeger, Washington, D.C.

64
The Letter. 1950. Welded steel, 37⅝ × 22⅞ × 9¼ inches. Munson-Williams-Proctor Institute, Utica, New York.

65
Growing Forms. 1939. Cast aluminum, 28 × 9 × 6 inches. Estate of the artist.

66
Royal Incubator. 1950. Steel, bronze, and silver, 37 × 38⅜ × 9⅞ inches. Estate of the artist.

67
Eagle's Lair. 1948. Steel and bronze, 33¾ × 17¼ × 13 inches. Estate of the artist.

68
Pillar of Sunday. 1945. Steel, painted pink, 30½ × 18 × 9½ inches. Estate of the artist.

69
Australia. 1951. Steel, painted brown, 79¾ × 107 × 16¾ inches. Collection William S. Rubin, New York.

70
Page from Sketchbook #41. 1944–1954. Archive IV/81.
71
The Hero. 1951–1952. Steel, painted red, 73⅝ × 25½ × 11¾ inches. Brooklyn Museum.
72
Sitting Printer. 1954. Bronze, 87½ × 15½ × 15 inches. Storm King Art Center, Mountainville, New York.
73
Cubi II. 1963. Stainless steel, 130½ × 36⅞ × 23⅞ inches. Estate of the artist.
74
Cubi VI. 1963. Stainless steel, 118⅛ × 29½ × 21¾ inches. Estate of the artist.
75
Tanktotem IX. 1960. Steel, painted blue, white, and red, 90¾ × 30¾ × 24⅛ inches. Estate of the artist.
76
Table Torso. 1942. Bronze, 10 × 4½ × 5⅝ inches. Rose Art Museum, Brandeis University, Waltham, Massachusetts.
77
Head as a Still Life II. 1942. Cast aluminum, 14 × 8½ × 4 inches. Estate of the artist.
78
Cathedral. 1950. Steel, painted brown, 34⅛ × 24½ × 17⅛ inches. Estate of the artist.
79
Sacrifice. 1950. Steel, painted red, 31⅝ × 19⅝ × 20⅞ inches. Estate of the artist.
80
Sentinel. 1961. Stainless steel, 106 × 23 × 16½ inches. Estate of the artist.
81
Voltri-Bolton XXIII. 1963. Steel, 69¼ × 24 × 25½ inches. Collection Miss Sara Dora Greenberg, New York.
82
Voltri-Bolton XXIII. (alternate view)
83
Albany XII. 1961. Steel, painted black, 30 × 14½ × 21¼ inches. Collection Mr. and Mrs. Stephen Paine, Boston.
84
Menand VI. 1963. Steel, treated with acid, 34¼ × 20¼ × 17¼ inches. Collection Mr. Wells Henderson, Gladwyne, Pennsylvania.
85
Voltri XVIII. 1962. Steel, 42⅜ × 40 × 32¾ inches. Estate of the artist.
86
Albany III. 1959. Steel, painted black, 26½ × 20 × 11¾ inches. Estate of the artist.
87
Ibram Lassaw. *Sculpture.* 1936. Plaster on pipe and wire armature, 36 inches. Collection of the artist.
88
Page from Notebook #12. Early 1940s. Archive III/604.
89
Page from Notebook #10. Early 1940s. Archive III/580.
90
Canopic Head. 1951. Steel, 42½ × 33 × 155⅛ inches. Estate of the artist.
91
Albany V. 1959. Steel, painted black, 22⅛ × 19¾ × 24⅜ inches. Private collection.
92
Circles and Arcs. 1961. Steel, painted white, green, and blue, 75 × 37¾ inches. Estate of the artist.
93
Cube III. 1961. Stainless steel, 95¾ × 33 × 19 inches. Estate of the artist.

94
Cube Totem. 1961. Stainless steel, 123½ × 90½ × 22 inches. Estate of the artist.
95
Lawrence Vail. *Bottle*. 1944. Mixed media, 16¼ inches. Collection Yvonne Hagen, New York.
96
René Magritte. *Bottle*. 1959. Painted bottle, 11¾ inches. Collection Harry Torczyner, New York.
97
Salvador Dali. *The Venus de Milo of the Drawers*. 1936. Painted bronze, 39⅜ inches. Galerie du Dragon, Paris.
98
André Masson. *Mannequin*. Installed at the international exhibition of Surrealism in 1936.
99
Roland Penrose. *The Last Voyage of Captain Cook*. 1936–1937. Mixed media, 27 × 26 × 34 inches. Collection of the artist.
100
Alberto Giacometti. *Cage*. 1931. Wood, 30 inches. Moderna Museet, Stockholm.
101
Spectre of War. 1944. Steel, painted black, 11¼ × 6 × 22 inches. Collection Mr. and Mrs. Jan de Graff, Portland, Oregon.
102
Jurassic Bird. 1945. Steel, painted white, 25⅝ × 35½ × 7¼ inches. Collection Dr. and Mrs. Paul T. Makler, Philadelphia.
103
False Peace Spectre. 1945. Bronze and steel, painted blue, 12½ × 27¼ × 10¾ inches. Collection Dr. and Mrs. Ralph Jessar, Philadelphia.
104
Spectre of Profit (Race for Survival). 1946. Steel and stainless steel, 18⅜ × 33½ × 6¼ inches. Collection Mr. and Mrs. Nathan Allen, Greenwich, Connecticut.
105
Page from Sketchbook #23. 1933–1945. Archive III/844.
106
Page from Sketchbook #23. 1933–1945. Archive III/880.
107
Reliquary House. 1945. Bronze and steel painted black, 12½ × 25½ × 11¾ inches. Collection Mr. and Mrs. David Mirvish.
108
Page from Sketchbook #23. 1933–1945. Archive III/828.
109
Page from Sketchbook #23. 1933–1945. Archive III/840.
110
Illustration in *Verve* 1, no. 4 (1939): 61. "L'Influence de la lune sur la teste des femmes." 17th century.
111
Page in *Verve* facing Fig. 110. Jean de Lery and Théodore de Bry. 16th century.
112
Untitled etching. 1942. Estate of the artist.
113
Uncatalogued page in the Archive. Early 1940s.
114
Perfidious Albion. 1945. Bronze, 14⅜ × 4½ × 2⅝ inches. Estate of the artist.
115
Medal for Dishonor: War Exempt Sons of the Rich. 1939–1940. Bronze, 10½ × 9 inches. Estate of the artist.
116
Page from Sketchbook #41. 1944–1954. Archive IV/88.

117

Home of the Welder. 1945. Steel, 21 × 17⅜ × 14 inches. Estate of the artist.

118a

Home of the Welder. (alternate view)

118b

Home of the Welder. (alternate view)

119

Landscape with Strata. 1946. Steel, bronze, and stainless steel, 16⅞ × 21 × 8½ inches. Estate of the artist.

120

Landscape with Strata. (alternate view)

121

Alexander Calder. *White Frame.* 1934. Wood panel, wire, and sheet metal, 90 × 108 inches. Collection of the artist.

122

Alexander Calder. *Thirteen Spines.* 1940. Sheet steel, rods, wire, and aluminum, 84 inches. Collection of the artist.

123

Ibram Lassaw. *Star Cradle.* 1949. Plastic and steel, 12 × 10 × 14 inches. Collection of the artist.

124

Blackburn: Song of an Irish Blacksmith. 1949–1950. Steel and bronze, 46¼ × 40¾ × 24 inches. Wilhelm Lehmbruch Museum, Duisberg, Germany.

125

Blackburn. (alternate view)

126

Voltri XVII. 1962. Steel, 95 × 31⅜ × 29¾ inches. Private collection.

127

Voltri XVII. (alternate view)

128

Voltri VIII. 1962. Steel, 79½ × 52½ × 33¾ inches. Estate of the artist.

129

Voltri VIII. (alternate view)

130

Picasso. *Personage.* 1935. Wood, string, and metal, 44¾ × 24 × 14 inches. Collection of the artist.

131

Picasso. *Baboon and Young.* 1951. Bronze, 21 inches. Museum of Modern Art, New York, Solomon Guggenheim Fund.

132

Agricola VIII. 1952. Steel and bronze, painted brown, 31¾ × 21½ × 18¾ inches. Estate of the artist.

133

Agricola VII. 1952. Steel and cast iron, painted red, 22⅞ × 13⅞ × 9½ inches. Collection Dr. and Mrs. Richard Kaplan, Philadelphia.

134

Agricola IX. 1952. Steel, 36¼ × 55¼ × 18 inches. Estate of the artist.

135

Tanktotem II. 1952–1953. Steel and bronze, 80½ × 49½ × 19 inches. Metropolitan Museum of Art, New York.

136

Voltri-Bolton X. 1962. Steel, 81¼ × 42 × 11¼ inches. Estate of the artist.

137

Volton XVIII. 1963. Steel, 110⅞ × 67⅛ × 15⅛ inches. Anonymous collection.

138

Picasso. *Musical Instrument.* 1914. Painted wood, 24 × 14½ inches. Collection of the artist.

139
March Sentinel. 1961. Stainless steel, 101¾ × 44 × 19¾ inches. Collection Dr. and Mrs. Paul T. Makler, Philadelphia.

140
Two Circle Sentinel. 1961. Stainless steel, 86¼ × 53 × 27½ inches. Collection Mr. and Mrs. Joseph Iseman, New York.

141
Cubi XXVI. 1965. Stainless steel, 119⅜ × 151¼ inches. Collection Philip M. Stern, Washington, D.C.

142
Cubi XXVII. 1965. Stainless steel, 111⅜ × 87¾ × 34 inches. Solomon Guggenheim Museum, New York.

143
Cubi XIX. 1964. Stainless steel, 113⅛ × 21¾ × 20 inches. Tate Gallery, London.

144
Cubi XXIV. 1964. Stainless steel, 114½ × 84¼ × 28¼ inches. Carnegie Institute of Art, Pittsburgh, Pennsylvania.

145
Cubi XXII. 1964. Stainless steel, 103¾ × 77¼ inches. Yale University Art Gallery, New Haven, Connecticut.

146
Cubi XII. 1963. Stainless steel, 110¼ inches. Joseph H. Hirshhorn Collection, New York.

147
Cubi I. 1963. Stainless steel, 124 × 34½ × 33½ inches. Detroit Institute of Art.

148
Cubi I. (alternate view)

Terminal Iron Works

1
David Smith in
the late 1930s.

Introduction

While this study was taking form, a rash of attacks on the critical procedures of formal analysis broke out in magazines of contemporary art criticism. After describing how, for various reasons, formalist criticism was unable to cope with the great profusion of styles that characterizes the artistic present, the authors of these articles all felt obliged to present an alternative. At that point, each in succession stepped up to the podium, bowed to the audience, and, gesturing proudly toward the wings, welcomed onto the critical stage . . . art history.[1] It seems that these writers see the art historian as the natural advocate of their own position. In their eyes, he is the spokesman for stylistic pluralism against the formalist's monolithic view of history. To the formalist's admitted partisanship, the historian can oppose a programmatic objectivity; in place of the formalist's unwillingness to discuss the content of works of art, he can offer an iconographic array as evidence of the preservation and development of the cultural themes of the past.

The systematic objectivity of the art historian has been likened to the efforts of a taxonomist to take a complete inventory of the living species that populate the earth and to relate them to one another by constructing a network of meaningful categories. In this view, the basic unit of investigation for the art historian is the life cycle of the individual, and the tool that the art historian generally uses for this is the monographic study of the lifework of a single member of the artistically significant community.[2]

A recent example of this deployment of art history as the advance guard of the irenic attitude directly concerns David Smith. Reviewing a recent publication of

[1] Thus Barbara Rose, after taking Clement Greenberg and Michael Fried to task for the presumptions she sees behind "a criticism that confines itself to a discussion of exclusively formal issues," advises: "Better suited to the complexity of the current situation . . . is perhaps a criticism based on a general field approach. . . . Already a synthetic criticism, which has no vested interest in ignoring subject matter or subject content is being practiced by a small group of art historians. . . ." ("The Politics of Art, Part I," *Artform* 6 [February 1968]: 32.) Much the same impulse directs the strident attack on Greenberg by Barbara Reise in *Studio International* (May-June 1968), pp. 254-257, 314-315.

[2] See, for example, George Kubler, *The Shape of Time* (New Haven: Yale University Press, 1962), pp. 5 ff.

Smith's writings, Lawrence Alloway quoted the sculptor's remark, "If you prefer one work over another, it is your privilege, but it does not interest me. The work is a statement of identity, it comes from a stream, it is related to my past works, the three or four works in process and the work yet to come."[3] Alloway then admonished, "This view of art as continuous with the history of production and of production as the graph of a life is Smith's demand on us. . . . It means that though we have, as Smith allowed, the option of doing what we want, we are warned of the irrelevance . . . of personal choice. . . . We are required to set the art in a system of definitions. In short, we are invited to work in an *art historical framework* if our acts of appreciation are to conform in any way to the artist's intentions."[4] (Emphasis added.)

The vulgarization these critics perform simultaneously on art history and on their own profession is to set the two endeavors at variance with one another. For in their most supreme examples the two practices are in fact complementary: the critic seeking to demonstrate the continuity of the most advanced art with that of the past and to locate the meaning of such objects in their revelation of that continuity;[5] the scholar acknowledging that certain objects or occurrences detach themselves from their historical background and strike him with their overwhelming importance, and that his task is to understand and to account for their sharpness of focus.

This, at any rate, is the art-historical model I have used for the present study of David Smith. Believing that his is the greatest body of work produced by any American sculptor, I find myself wanting to explain this conviction. Further, I feel the need to advocate that select group of objects out of the whole of his work that most clearly testify to his preeminence. Therefore, while a complete listing of Smith's sculpture would number nearly seven hundred items, I have dealt explicitly with only about

[3] The quotation from Smith appears at the beginning of *David Smith by David Smith,* ed. Cleve Gray (New York: Holt, Rinehart & Winston, 1968), p. 17.
[4] Lawrence Alloway, "David Smith and Modern Sculpture," *Arts* 43 (February 1969): 36.
[5] This point is made again and again in the writings of Clement Greenberg (see "Modernist Painting," *Arts Yearbook* 4 [1961]), and Michael Fried (see "Shape as Form: Frank Stella's New Paintings," *Artforum* 5 [November 1966]: 27, fn. 11; and "Art and Objecthood," *Artforum* 5 [Summer 1967]).

forty. But these forty comprise a core of work exemplifying Smith's particular attitude toward sculpture, an attitude fully embodied in the masterpieces of his career,
and which I hope to prove he held fundamentally unchanged throughout his entire
artistic lifetime. If this be the case, it follows that in characterizing this attitude a chronological study will explain very little. Rather, it might obscure the fact that from first
to last Smith clung to and worried a single set of issues with an impressive single-
mindedness.

The writers who have approached Smith's work from the point of view of chronology
have met with exactly those dangers. Insofar as they have tried to explain his art in
terms of its origins, they have seen him as reenacting the development of twentieth-
century style. They stress, for example, that a "relation to Cubism and collage must
be kept formally in mind for a full understanding of Smith's art,"[6] or that "the importance of Surrealism as a formative influence in Smith's development should not be
underestimated."[7] This kind of explanation threatens to bury the significance of Smith's
sculpture under an avalanche of styles and mannerisms. Thus one writer insists, "From
Cubism and from the Constructivism which grew out of it, [Smith] drew his formal
syntax; from Surrealism, a vein of fantasy that permitted a free range of symbolic and
imagistic invention; and from Expressionism, a gestural freedom that allowed an
unflagging energy to penetrate and animate these elements of fantasy and construction, and carry them into new expressive arrangements."[8]

In the course of the following study, I hope it will become clear why statements like
these are deeply misleading. Against the testimony that a brute chronological succession of works provides, I will set out three different types of evidence. One will be
a characterization of the formal impulse of Smith's art and the way in which that impulse was critically directed against the essential conservatism of modern sculpture.
Another is the specific set of images Smith repeatedly drew on and how they reveal
the content of his art. The third is a body of biographical and documentary detail

[6] Hilton Kramer, "David Smith," *Arts* 34 (February 1960): 22.
[7] Jane Harrison Cone, "David Smith," *Artforum* 5 (Summer 1967): 74.
[8] Hilton Kramer, *David Smith* (Los Angeles: Los Angeles County Museum of Art, 1966), p. 3.

intended to support the claims made by the first two. This documentation also suggests the difficulties that beset any simple notion of symbiosis between David Smith and his historical context. In short, I have tried to suspend my preconceptions about art-historical method and to let the considerations of this book be dictated by what I take to be the meaning of the work itself.

The Core of Objects

The Surface of Objects

David Smith was fifty-nine when, in the spring of 1965, the carryall he was driving went out of control and, spinning sideways off a Vermont road, crushed him to death. The truck had been integral to Smith's life at his farmland studio at Bolton Landing in the mountains above Lake George. He had used it to haul and maintain the heavy equipment that filled the shop where he made his sculpture, and he had used it to place the enormous finished works in the cleared fields around his house.

Smith had left New York City for Bolton Landing in 1940, bringing with him an ambition to make great sculpture, nurtured by the city and the artists he had known there; bringing also a name for the farm—the Terminal Iron Works—transplanted from the noisy waterfront shop in Brooklyn where Smith had first welded sculpture. When Smith died, his ambition was in one sense gratified. Populating the fields at the Terminal Iron Works were the greatest sculptures ever produced by an American artist. But the other part of ambition is the desire for fame. In 1965 Smith's reputation had not really reached beyond the fierce admiration of his fellow artists, a few critics, most notably Clement Greenberg and Hilton Kramer, and a very small part of the general art public.

Now, five years after his death, Smith's reputation is commensurate with his ambition. In this country and in Europe, major museums and enthusiastic collectors have avidly reaped the fields at Bolton Landing of the harvest of a thirty-year-long career. As with almost everything else in his life, Smith would have been of two minds about that. The sculpture standing in the fields at Bolton Landing had represented a kind of freedom. The place is now stripped and the sculpture possessed by others. Even the newly grown size of the reputation has something unfinished and raw about it. For the massive steel sculptures Smith made were invested with a complex meaning, and Smith's desire to have his work seen by others was first of all a desire to be understood.

In the early 1950s David Smith's work appeared on the American cultural horizon as the counterpart in sculpture to the Abstract Expressionists in painting. In the public mind they were all linked by a shared engagement in a heroic struggle with material. A Colossus astride the scrap pile of heavy industry, Smith was pictured as the artist-welder who could bend steel to the dictates of his individual will. He was a Titan. He was Vulcan.[1] He was whatever mythological personage journalists could find to announce the newness, the vitality, and, most of all, the independence of postwar American art.

There were times when Smith himself expressed contempt for these characterizations, which, in their effort to give the public ease of access to a new and difficult world of form, ended by sentimentalizing both that world and its creators.[2] But for the most part, Smith seemed to like playing the role of Titan. He even encouraged its elaboration into myth by choosing to make public only certain details of his life. His written statements, too, sounded like proclamations designed to serve the picture of the hero-artist. It was a picture of a man who would allow his entire identity to be lodged in the body of his sculpture, which he would neither rationalize nor judge, but which he was content to be judged by.[3] Smith repeatedly refused to explain his art. To any question about the meaning of a particular sculpture, he would reply evasively: "I've made it because it comes closer to saying who I am than any other method I could use.[4] Again and again, Smith maintained simply that his work was his "identity."

According to this view of art as the manifestation of identity, there is supposed to be a direct relation between the work and the emotional life of its maker. Just as a man does not calculate the form of a grimace, so the artist who is registering his life through

[1] Cleve Gray, "David Smith," *Art in America* 54 (January 1966): 23, and Giovanni Carandente, *Voltron* (Philadelphia: University of Pennsylvania Press, 1964), p. 5.

[2] Across the cover of a magazine with nationwide circulation in which there was an article on several of the American sculptor-welders, including himself, Smith scrawled his impression of the kind of popularizations that sell magazines. He wrote, "Australia p. 58—Fire shit." See "Sculptors with Fire," *Look*, August 12, 1952. This copy of the magazine is in the Smith Archive in the Archives of American Art in Detroit.

[3] Gray has quoted Smith as repeatedly saying to him, "I never stop to decide what's good and what isn't—I just do the work—I don't judge it. . . ." ("David Smith," p. 26). Gray also used Smith's disclaimer—"If you prefer one work over another, it is your privilege, but it does not interest me. The work is my identity"—as an epigraph to the book on Smith that he edited. See Introduction, fn. 3.

[4] Archive IV/812. The microfilms of Smith's papers and sketchbooks are now on deposit at the Archives of American Art in Detroit. The roman numeral indicates the microfilm reel, and the arabic number the frame on which the cited material appears.

2a
David Smith working
at Bolton Landing.
2b
David Smith at Voltri.
3a
David Smith in one of
his studios at Bolton
Landing.
3b
David Smith in the
basement of the house
at Bolton Landing.

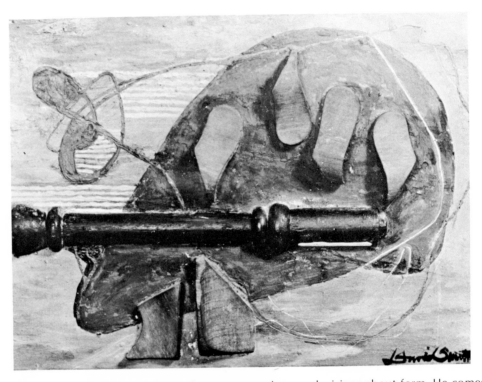

4
Collage. 1932. Estate
of the artist.

gesture, no matter how abstract, does not struggle over decisions about form. He comes
by his formal decisions, he would say, naturally and without cost.

"The first constructions that grew off my canvas were wood," Smith remembers, "somewhere between 1930 and 1933. Then there was an introduction of metal lines and
found forms. The next step changed the canvas to the base of the sculpture. And then
I became a sculptor who painted his images."[5] Although he avoided any specific discussion of his work, Smith liked to sketch the general profile of his own artistic history;
he did it with the abrupt, abbreviated strokes of someone who draws from the shoulder,
with his full arm. He wrote these descriptions again and again, and each time the development sounded easier, the transitions from one state to the next more effortless.
While he elaborated into the proportions of a myth the day-to-day struggles of his
personal biography—his childhood, his relations to others, his fight to gain the time
to work at his sculpture—he smoothed out the kinks and turnings in his artistic autobiography until he finally erased them. From Cubist painting to construction, from
construction to freestanding sculpture in a little over three years: it sounds so unproblematic because, like any historical simplification, it records solutions, not problems.
First of all, the Cubists were never able to translate the discoveries made with their
early relief constructions into large-scale, freestanding sculpture; and for Smith himself
the translation occupied fully half his career.

If this is so, it is because Smith did in fact labor over a single set of formal issues.
The full scope of that labor will be missed if we simply accept Smith's formula about
the course of his development or if we honor his injunction against examining the
content of his sculpture. For that content is suggestive in a way that Smith's own written statements are not. Growing out of a particular set of images that Smith repeated
from the beginning to the end of his career, it seems to bridge the mute privacy of
Smith's personal preoccupations and his ambitions for a fully articulate, public, formal
language. The complicated terrain of Smith's sculpture can be explored by means of

[5]"David Smith," in *The Artist's Voice*, ed. Katherine Kuh (New York: Harper & Row, 1962), p. 224.

5
Construction.
1932. Wood, wire, and
plaster, 18½ × 5 ×
9½ inches. Estate of
the artist.

the clues these images provide; by examining them, a standard of meaning can be constructed to test assumptions about the direction of Smith's formal development. And this test must be applied not only to the theories of the critics and historians who have written about Smith's work but to the characterizations furnished by Smith himself.

In the second chapter I will inspect the bridge between Smith's imagery and his exertions to forge a new formal language. But I will start by examining the dimensions of that language, for I want to show how deeply it was bent on expressing the disjunction between a sculptural object and its observer, although they are inevitably present in the same space.

In the masterpieces of David Smith's maturity, the very features that affirm the sculpture as a physical object—shape, surface, structure—simultaneously establish the peculiar elusiveness of the work. Unlike some kinetic sculpture, it is not the meeting ground for two sets of contradictory impressions, one vision of it as dense and obdurate, the other as ephemeral and in flux. Smith believed in the viability of the conventions of traditional sculpture. This impelled him to make one and the same set of elements the vehicle for establishing both modes. The sculpture's deepest meaning is the discovery of this continuity. As we survey the course of his career, we see this idea change from a theme that the works seem merely to illustrate to the fully integrated formal directive that a major sculpture like *Zig IV* (Fig. 6) seems effortlessly to carry.

Zig IV projects eight feet high out toward and over the viewer. It can be described as a collection of fragments—huge cylindrical tubes split into shallow arcs—projecting off a sloping plane balanced delicately on one point near the viewer's feet. The presence of this plane and the way it seems to be a ground for the other elements in the sculpture suggest that the work can be read within the normal conventions of sculptural relief. The viewer expects that the surface will operate like the plane of a picture: it will be the matrix of a traditional illusionistic field. But the plane contradicts this function by appearing to truncate the sculpture, so that the spectator feels that half the work is shielded from view. He can experience parts of *Zig IV* only as fragments of a whole entity extending beyond the boundary of his vision.[6]

Why would Smith do this? Why would he build into a sculpture the idea of a relief space and then deny it by simultaneously suggesting that the sculpture is composed of two intersecting elements, one of which obscures half the other?

We can move closer to explaining the apparent paradox embodied in *Zig IV* if we realize that Smith is dealing in this work with two alternate ways of organizing the visual data that surround everyone. On the one hand, he alludes to the patterns of intelligibility that are the heart of pictorial thought in, for example, perspective systems or narrative relief. On the other hand, he recalls the palpable objects that are the substance of physical experience. But it has been shown that *both* the pictorial and literal modes of perceiving are aborted in *Zig IV*. For *Zig IV* is a new kind of object, whose main characteristic is that it can be grasped neither literally nor figuratively.

The physical presence of *Zig IV* eludes us. Unlike a man-made or natural object, the sculpture does not appear whole and complete. We cannot run our fingers around it to trace its contours and define its shape. The startling fact is that although *Zig IV* is all boundaries, made completely of curving walls and angled planes, these contours bound nothing, not even a comprehensible volume of air. We have only a visual display of surfaces slipping past one another, throwing each other into relief even as they slide past the sight of the spectator moving in front of the aloof construction. Given the ambivalent character of *Zig IV*, we cannot grasp it imaginatively.

Intellectually, the work is equally elusive. The plane against which we see the curving walls of *Zig IV*, the plane that, opening out to us, guarantees their visibility in the first place, does not organize the elements into a comprehensible pattern. In fact, our sense

[6] There are many "clues" in the sculpture that promote the illusion of incompleteness. For one, small steel ridges fastened to the underside of the plane, which are made visible because they extend slightly beyond its edges, assert themselves as the visual counterpart to the ridges of metal that delineate areas at the front of the sculpture. Or the way the base of the work—a small length of structural steel shaped like an inverted T in section—lies mostly behind the diamond-shaped plane. But at the very front of the work a corner of this base actually pokes through to the surface, acting out at one point the situation that the entire sculpture so potently suggests.

6
Zig IV. 1961. Steel,
painted yellow-ochre,
95⅜ × 84¼ × 76
inches. Collection
Lincoln Center for the
Performing Arts, New
York.
7
Zig IV. (alternate
views)

that the piece is somehow truncated and that half of it is hidden derives most strongly from the absence of a way to relate the elements in the work to some familiar convention. The continuous flat plane of *Zig IV* signals the presence of the other planes but does not organize them, making them present to vision alone.[7]

Insofar as *Zig IV* is all boundary and all skin, it appears to us as surfaceness itself, stripped from the object that would normally function as its support. *Zig IV* involves a kind of visual paradox, for its apparent availability to the viewer is contradicted by the absence of a possessable object.

The Core of
Objects: Picasso,
Gonzalez, Boccioni

As early as 1933, Smith had focused his energies on the notion of an elusive object. His primary insight grew out of an instinctive refusal to erect his sculpture around a central spine. By rejecting the idea of the spine or inner core he had freed his own work from the formal conservatism that persisted even in the most open of the European constructed sculptures of the 1930s.

A comparison will make this immediately clear: it is between Picasso's 1930 *Construction in Metal Wire* (Fig. 9) and Smith's *Aerial Construction* (Fig. 8) of six years later. The Picasso is relevant as the type of work that is presumably a direct antecedent to Smith's sculpture, for a variant on it was reproduced in the issue of *Cahiers d'art* that his friend John Graham showed Smith in the summer of 1932.[8] It was this sculpture that catalyzed

[7]Clement Greenberg was the first to see modern sculpture in terms of "visibility," "opticality," and an experience in three dimensions addressed to "eyesight alone." His seminal discussions of these ideas are in "The New Sculpture," "Collage," and "Modernist Sculpture, Its Pictorial Past," collected in *Art and Culture* (Boston: Beacon Press, 1962). Michael Fried's writings on the English sculptor Anthony Caro have extended the ground originally covered by Greenberg. Fried examines the way in which composition and the use of color have been reconceived by modernist sculptors. See "Anthony Caro," *Art International* 6 (September 1963): 68–72, and "New Work by Anthony Caro," *Artforum* 5 (February 1967): 46–47.

[8]Although Smith attributed to various years his encounter with the issue of *Cahiers d'art* (no. 4 [1929]) that bore the reproduction of Picasso's *Project for a Sculpture in Metal Wire,* Dorothy Dehner claims that it took place during a visit with the Grahams in the summer of 1932. Smith's published autobiographical notations tend to confirm this. *David Smith by David Smith,* ed. Cleve Gray (New York: Holt, Rinehart & Winston, 1968), p. 25.

8
Aerial Construction.
1936. Iron, painted
terra-cotta, 9¼ × 31
× 9 inches. Joseph
H. Hirshhorn Collec-
tion, New York.
9
Picasso. *Construction
in Metal Wire.* 1929–
1930. Iron, 20 × 16½
inches. Collection of
the artist.

Smith's own prior knowledge of welding into a recognition that he could make major sculpture from a medium of constructed metal. It also putatively served Smith as a model for a radically abstract sculpture based on the notions of transparency and drawing in space. *Aerial Construction* is indeed like the Picasso in that a network of line is produced by welding together metal rods. It might also be argued that the two works state their abstractness—their unlikeness to nature—in similar ways, by the velleities they both possess toward simple geometric figures: in the case of the Smith, a truncated pyramid whose rectangular base is defined by the four connected horizontal rods which the whole structure sits on; in the case of the Picasso, an elongated prism. But this argument would be wrong, because the crucial point of difference between Smith and Picasso in these works is precisely over the adherence to simple geometry.

 Indeed, Picasso *does* construct such a simple form, and the theme of his sculpture, one might almost say its point, is the comprehensibility of a complex figure in terms of its geometry. Picasso's *Construction* depicts a charioteer standing erect, outstretched arms grasping the reins of a missing horse. Because of the unitary completeness of the figure with its gesture, despite the fact that part of the figurative ensemble is gone, it seems that Picasso is explicitly referring to the *Charioteer of Delphi,* or in any event to the idea that even in fragment Greek statues strike the viewer with a peculiar conviction about the wholeness of the object. An oval or shield form states the torso of Picasso's charioteer, while four extremely planar sides define the sculpture as a whole and seem to allude to the blocklike character of archaic Greek figures. Against this perception of the classical referent, the sculpture pits a newfound transparency, which seeks to expose a schematic structure at the heart of normally opaque, solid objects. For the viewer can see how all the sides of the sculpture are generated by the initial proposition of a core shape: the skeleton of the charioteer stated as an elongated triangle, which Picasso extends and elaborates into the complex network of relations that make up the prismatic form of the sculpture.

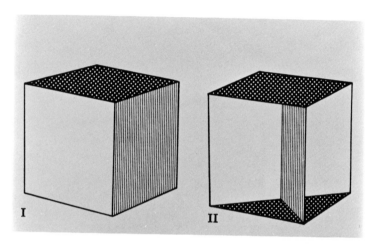

10
Naum Gabo. Diagram showing volumetric (I) and stereometric (II) cubes. Published in 1937 in *Circle*. Reprinted in *Naum Gabo* (Cambridge: Harvard University Press, 1957), p. 168.

In an article setting forth the precepts of Constructivism,[9] Gabo was to restate the same principle in the form of a simple diagram of two cubes (Fig. 10): the first a closed volume, the second a stereometric form defined by two square planes intersecting at right angles. What the second, opened cube revealed for Gabo was not merely the space ordinarily displaced by closed volumes, but the core of the geometric object, laid bare as the principle of intersection itself, making the figure comprehensible much the way a geometric theorem isolates and makes available essential propositions about solid objects.

Turning to *Aerial Construction*, it is immediately obvious that this insistence on intersection and on a core, of which the sides are logical projections, is simply rejected. Although Smith has harmoniously repeated many triangular shapes throughout the work, the logical relationships among them remain obscure. They do not form the sides of a figure that is in any way symmetrical about a central axis, nor are they the fins of a stereometrically created whole. Because of this, the viewer cannot feel he has any guarantee about the order that will obtain among these shapes should he examine the work from a different angle. This lack of certainty does not arise from the fact that Picasso is depicting something—a human figure—and Smith is not. In fact, Smith is presenting a still life whose dominant element is a guitar. But instead of allowing the shape of the guitar to generate the shape of the sculpture, Smith simply appends the musical instrument to the surface of the sculpture in such a way that we cannot tell where its defining contour begins and ends. Because no definite shape can be assigned to the guitar, and none is possessed by the sculpture as a whole, there seems to be no way to project what the work will look like from another angle. The absence of generating core and enclosing shape leads to the conclusion that Smith means something entirely different by *his* use of transparency than Picasso did by his own.

Because the question of the core is crucial for understanding Smith's radical reorientation of both the formal and thematic content of his sculpture, we need to come to terms with what the core meant to Smith's European predecessors. And that means

[9] Naum Gabo, "Sculpture: Carving and Construction in Space," reprinted in *Naum Gabo* (Cambridge: Harvard University Press, 1957), p. 168.

seeing how the birth of an open welded idiom in the art of Picasso and Gonzalez was an affirmation rather than a denial of the way artists in the mid-twentieth century viewed the enterprise of sculpture. That Picasso in the 1930s should have shifted his efforts to the basically naïve, epistemological concerns of this age-old tradition is especially surprising in the light of his revolutionary break with it during the years of Analytic Cubism. Yet undeniably that is what Picasso did, so that his sculptural statements in the thirties curiously ignore his own first three-dimensional declarations (1912–1916) and respond instead to problems raised by men like Boccioni and Gabo.

Therefore, even while the vocabulary of metal wires and rods pointed toward the idea of transparency and openness, both Picasso and Gonzalez, in their welded sculpture, furtively suggested the a priori unity of the simple, closed object by maintaining a vertebral infrastructure for their animals or dancers or heads. From this core sprang the linear members of their "transparent" or "open" forms; but no matter how attenuated or apparently weightless these elements became, the old idea of the sculptural solid was retained, for neither Picasso nor Gonzalez ever relinquished the kind of coherence a structural spine implies. We have only to look at a sculpture by Gonzalez from his 1935 exhibition (Fig. 11) to see how resolutely he assembles one scythelike metal edge and one disc-shaped plate into an intimation of the full volume of a human head. With a newfound economy, Gonzalez fashions the profile of the cranium out of slender metal elements coerced into the shape of a crescent. Perpendicular to this linear profile, a flat, encrusted disc states the breadth of the face, and two graphic elements, a metal U and a metal V, locate eyes and mouth. To Gabo's Constructivist lesson that two intersecting planes are enough to register the entire space that would be displaced by a solid, cubic mass, Gonzalez's *Head* adds the dimension of expressive gesture. But, significantly, it is a gesture that depends for its effect on maintaining a schematic description of the head's volume. It is as if this skeletal geometry of arc and plate were laying bare the structural essence of the ordinarily closed organic form. Any other Gonzalez of the 1930s, or any Picasso for that matter, would equally reveal this insistence on volume as a projection of a core and this concern for the generation of

11
Julio Gonzalez. *Head.*
1935. Wrought iron,
17¾ inches. Museum
of Modern Art, New
York.

12
Umberto Boccioni,
*Development of a
Bottle in Space.* 1912.
Bronze, 15 × 24
inches. Museum of
Modern Art, New
York.

whole entities from the inside out. Surrealist sculpture followed where Picasso and Gonzalez led, but while Picasso and Gonzalez sought to expose the interior core of the normally opaque volume, Giacometti and the other Surrealist sculptors reveled in the idea of formal secrets hidden within the placidly solid objects.

A survey of the "radical" sculpture produced in the first three decades of this century shows a surprising conceptual unity, for all its diversity of style. It seems consistently to have been made in an effort to defeat the implacable solidity of objects. This is true whether, as in the case of Constructivism and the welded metal sculpture of Gonzalez, it labored to expose the object's interior to a probing x-ray vision or whether, as in Giacometti's or Arp's objects, it was based on the mysterious privacy at the object's core. Since both procedures seem to have assumed that the meaning of the object lay at its core, it is fair to say that both implied that normal human perception was a kind of cheat, inadequate for a total comprehension of three-dimensional objects. What I would like, then, to put forward as the persistent meaning of the core is that it represents an ideological position that makes sculpture an investigatory tool in the service of knowledge.

The idea that the object's surface is a projection from its unseen and mysterious core did not originate with the sculpture of the 1930s. It became the major theme of those sculptors who operated around the central figures of Cubism in the late teens, setting themselves the epistemological problem of the duality between the inside and the outside of objects. It was a conceptual issue that came into art garbed in the robes of an idealist philosophy. It can be felt most insistently in a sculpture like Boccioni's 1912 *Development of a Bottle in Space* (Fig. 12).

In this work the bottle is presented as a succession of concentric cores. We can read from its silhouette its total shape as a bottle: the upright sides of the cylindrical body, the inward tapering of the shoulders, and the slender shaft of the neck. But at various places this exterior shell is cut away, so that beneath its solid facade can be seen other, more interior profiles, similarly shaped. At the very inside of the work, presented as the goal of the viewer's exploratory gaze, is a concavity that is also bottle-shaped. Unlike the positive, convex skin at the periphery of the sculpture, this innermost bottle is a negative shape, a hollow. But it is a definite core extending upward through the interior, like a fictive spine around which the other, more exterior bottle revolves in a spiral movement. It is the "real" shape of the bottle as given in appearance.

Boccioni is saying, then, that there are two bottles: a real one, which we don't see ordinarily but which we know conceptually—just as we know cubes or spheres, geometric abstractions that, when they are embodied in real objects, cannot have the transparency that shines through the objects of thought; and a less real bottle, the bottle seen from the outside and therefore seen only partially. Boccioni is responding to the "Cubist" problem as it was spelled out by Gleizes and Metzinger, who called on simultaneity to project the complete object in terms of its "successive appearances."[10] In other words, it is the Cubist problem reconstructed from the lectures of Henri Bergson, rather than the quite different one suggested by the canvases of Braque or Picasso.

In addressing himself to the real and the less real bottle, Boccioni is talking about the viewer's supposed capacity to "analyze" his perception into components, to synthesize the object from what he sees and what he knows. He is responding to the cheat that is vision from a fixed viewpoint. After all, he says with Bergson, if I say I see a bottle and am referring to what I see of the object over there from my fixed position here, I am lying. I really see only its outside surface and of that, only the part directly facing me.[11] I do not see its back or its inside. But my experience is not constructed from fragments of that kind, because objects for me are full of possible views of their reverse sides, their centers, their "realities." It is to this intellectual suspicion of fraud that Boccioni responded both pictorially and sculpturally with a diagrammatic rendering of Bergson's notion of duration. The bottle rotated 360 degrees around its core is the

---

[10] ". . . the fact of moving round an object to seize from it several successive appearances, which fused into a single image, reconstitute it in time, will no longer make reasoning people indignant." Albert Gleizes and Jean Metzinger, "Cubism" (1912), reprinted in *Modern Artists on Art*, ed. Robert Herbert (Englewood Cliffs, N.J.: Prentice-Hall, 1965).

[11] See Thompson Clark, "Seeing Surface and Physical Objects," in *Philosophy in America*, ed. Max Black (Ithaca: Cornell University Press, 1965). Michael Fried called my attention to this essay in his article, "Shape as Form: Frank Stella's New Paintings," *Artforum* 5 (November 1966).

bottle seen from all its possible views. The viewer is given the object in what Boccioni saw as a new kind of completeness.

Boccioni substitutes for the theoretical poverty of the fixed viewpoint, then, a fullness of perception that is idealist in kind. Yet from a historical perspective one becomes skeptical of this fullness, for it suggests that the viewer is made into a disembodied intelligence circulating through space, a constructive consciousness whose viewpoint on the world and its contents is one of omniscience. The sculptor's ambition is to give to the spectator the bottle as it would be seen from everywhere; the result is to present it as it would be seen from nowhere.[12] And despite Boccioni's Futurist claims, the idealism of this omniscient point of view is a continuation of the idealist tradition of nineteenth-century academic art.[13] Not only does it permeate the subject matter of official nineteenth-century painting—as in the various strategies used by salon painters to elaborate the representation of moments in a historical or psychological narrative into the illusion of the viewer's mastery or control over the action portrayed—but omniscience permeates academic classicism as a formal ideal. It is summed up, for example, in the prescriptive writings of Hildebrand: "All detail of form must unite in a more comprehensive form. All separate judgments of depth must enter into a unitary, all-inclusive judgment of

[12] See Maurice Merleau-Ponty, *The Phenomenology of Perception* (London: Routledge and Kegan Paul, 1962), pp. 67 ff.

[13] The assumption that the viewer can be at the inside, can know (see) everything, deserts the idea of a fixed point of view and returns to one that is at base academic. The idea that with the defeat of rational or traditional perspective in Cubism, modernism itself embraced the omniscient point of view is, of course, false. The Cubist paintings of Picasso and·Braque never invited the viewer to move around or penetrate objects, or to experience reality in a durational manner. Instead they presented objects in a piecemeal fashion, so that the organization of any three-dimensional whole would have to depend on understanding the continuity of the picture's surface, not the object's independent shape. The object could no longer be imagined from another point of view. It had been absorbed by a system whose defining characteristic is that the amount of increased information yielded to the viewer as he moves around it is null. This simultaneous vision of the object and the surface does not loosen the viewer from his fixed point of view, allowing him to escape his own materiality and move in spirit around the object. Instead, it reinforces the fixity of the viewer's stance, giving him with increased palpability the sense of illusionism itself. See Greenberg, *Art and Culture*, pp. 76-77.

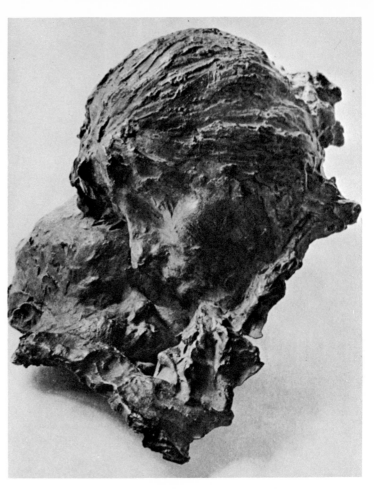

depth. So that ultimately the entire richness of a figure's form stands before us as a backward continuation of one simple plane."[14] According to Hildebrand, the sculptor had to guarantee that when the beholder took up his stance opposite a statue he would know at a glance all the possibilities of shape and gesture that the figure could offer. For Boccioni, too, the enterprise of sculpture was based on the same idealist premise.

To couple Boccioni with Adolf Hildebrand is to reinsert the Futurist into the nineteenth-century tradition of relief sculpture, which at first must seem totally antithetical to Boccioni's ambitions to integrate the freestanding object with the actual space that surrounded it. Yet if we refuse to take his statements about sculpture at face value and look instead at his work, we see that the real precedent for the *Bottle* is to be found precisely in the realm of the nineteenth-century relief. For it is there that we first find artists not only trying to provide the viewer with sensory information about the unseen (and of course unseeable) sides of whole objects but making it a major sculptural theme. Given the unassailable frontality of relief, such information about the concealed side of the figure had to come simultaneously with the perception of its front. Increasingly throughout nineteenth-century relief sculpture this information was supplied by the programmatic inclusion of actual shadows cast on the relief ground by the raised figurative elements. Thus Medardo Rosso's *Mother and Child Sleeping* (Fig. 13) contains, not two, but three figurative elements. The first is the gently swollen circle of the infant head. The second is the voluptuous fabric of the side of the female face in which the concave and convex forms of forehead, cheek, and mouth are gathered into the simple contour of the profile. The third, which lies between them, is the field of shadow cast by the mother onto the face of the child. What is striking about this shadow is that it does not function, as we would expect, by injecting a

[14] Adolf von Hildebrand, *The Problem of Form* (New York: Stechart, 1907), p. 95. Following the passage quoted in the text, Hildebrand says: "Whenever this is not the case, the unitary pictorial effect of the figure is lost. A tendency is then felt to clarify what we cannot perceive from our present point of view, by a change of position. Thus we are driven all around the figure without ever being able to grasp it once in its entirety."

13
Medardo Rosso.
*Mother and Child
Sleeping*. 1883. Bronze,
13⅞ inches. Collection
Cesare Fasola,
Florence.

14
Medardo Rosso. *The
Golden Age*. 1886.
Wax over plaster,
17 inches. Galleria
d'Arte Moderna,
Rome.
15 Medardo Rosso.
The Flesh of Others.
1883. Wax over
plaster, 21 inches.
Whereabouts un-
known.

quantity of open space into the clenched forms of the sculpture or by serving the organizational purpose of a fulcrum of darkness on which to balance two light-drenched volumes. Instead, the shadow produces insistent visual testimony about the other side of the woman's head. To the exposed surfaces of the faces, which carry the continual reminder of the sculptor's touch as he modeled them, the shadow adds the fact of the most intense and poignant area of touch: the contact between the hidden cheek of the mother and the buried forehead of the child. It is as though Rosso felt that it was not enough simply to excavate figures from the ground of the relief; he also supplies data about the realms of interaction so immersed within the material of the sculpture that neither the probe of his fingers nor our gaze could reach them. It is surely part of Rosso's meaning that beyond the brilliance of his modeling and the coruscation of the light insistently opening and penetrating his surfaces lies an unseeable area of the form about which he is compelled to report.[15]

Far from being an art-historical foundling, Rosso's need to render the invisible sides

[15] What can be seen in the 1883 *Mother and Child Sleeping* is also manifest in *Flesh of Others* from the same year and in *The Golden Age,* 1886. In both these works, cast shadow is a datum of the sculptural ensemble. Although to my knowledge there is no photograph of *Mother and Child Sleeping* taken by the sculptor himself, there exist several original photographs of the two other sculptures from Rosso's own hand. (See Mino Borghi, *Medardo Rosso* [Milan: Edizioni del Milione, 1950], Plates 11, 14, and 15.) They are photographs that emphasize to an even greater extent that the function of internal cast shadow was to gesture toward the unseeable sides of objects. (See Fig. 14.) In her monograph, Margaret S. Barr notes that "Rosso insisted that his sculpture be reproduced only from photographs taken by himself because he felt that his impressions should be seen in one light and at one angle. . . ." (*Medardo Rosso* [New York: Museum of Modern Art, 1963], p. 46.) On a photograph of *Flesh of Others*, Rosso wrote that it was the first of his sculptures "around which one could not walk." (Barr, *Rosso*, p. 67, fn. 35.) It is clear that the single viewing point of the relief tradition is operative in Rosso's consideration of sculpture, and that it is tied conceptually to the effects of light and shadow. In the middle 1890s the question of the cast shadow became an even more dominant theme in Rosso's work. Barr describes this visual phenomenon as "the checkmark effect that a figure forms with its own shadow" (p. 43) and wants to see it in terms of an impulse that is Impressionist in kind. The context in which I have discussed Rosso's use of the cast shadow suggests that an Impressionist fusion of object and atmosphere does not adequately account for its meaning within the sculpture at this time.

of objects is a legitimate product of nineteenth-century relief.[16] From Thomas Eakins's
bronzes of contemporary genre (Fig. 16) to Hildebrand's antiquarian plaques (Fig. 17)
there is a unifying formal impulse. Whether we are speaking of an ardent realist or
a dogmatic classicist, we see that, in the work of both, forms are marshaled so that the
shadows they cast would direct the viewer's attention to the buried and unseen sides.

If we move one generation forward, from Rosso's figures to Boccioni's *Bottle,* we
see that Rosso's impulse to carry the viewer around the head and into the crevices of
the ground is simply brought to a logical climax by the Futurist. The *Bottle's* rigid
frontality (for its insistence on a relief arrangement is particularly striking) sets up a way
for the viewer to surmount his physical fixity before the objects of his perception.
Theoretically, the core and the spiral oppose to this fixity the dynamism of the beholder's constructive intellect.

The "Cubist" constructors of the late teens seconded Boccioni's conception of the
sculptural problem. In their combined concern for a relief plane and a structural core,
Lipchitz, Gabo, and Pevsner circumvented the sculptural direction that Picasso was
fitfully exploring during the years 1912–1916. For although the work Picasso did at that
time raised the question of relief, it constituted a complete refutation of what might

[16] Quite obviously these remarks do not apply to Rodin's *Gates of Hell,* which must qualify at one
and the same time as the most famous and most atypical relief of the nineteenth century. The dif-
ferences between Rosso and Rodin are numerous and profound. I shall limit myself to saying that
the role of shadow cast by figures onto each other or onto the ground of the relief is utterly different
from what I have been claiming as a general principle for Rodin's contemporaries. Cast shadow
here seems to emphasize the isolation and detachment of full-round figures from the relief ground
and in so doing to enforce our sense of the ground as an object in its own right, solid like any
other object, rather than the conventionally transparent matrix of illusionism. In addition, shadow
bears witness to the sense that the figures are intentionally fragmented and necessarily incomplete
rather than only perceptually incomplete, as in Rosso. Albert Elsen does not discuss shadow as a
formal element in *The Gates,* but he does refer to the question of a viewing point, which I have
been discussing in relation to the character of shadow. "The scale of the sculptures," he says, "is
inconsistent if one assumes that they were meant to be graded from a single point of view. In
meditating upon the door, Rodin may have decided, however, that the figures should be independent
of any single, outside, ideal observer, and that the world within the portal should instead be self-
enclosed." (*Rodin* [New York: Museum of Modern Art, 1963], p. 41.)

18
Picasso. *Guitar*. 1912.
Paper, 13¼ × 6½
inches. Collection of
the artist.
19
Picasso, *Guitar*. 1914.
Painted lead, 38 ×
26¼ inches. Collection
of the artist.

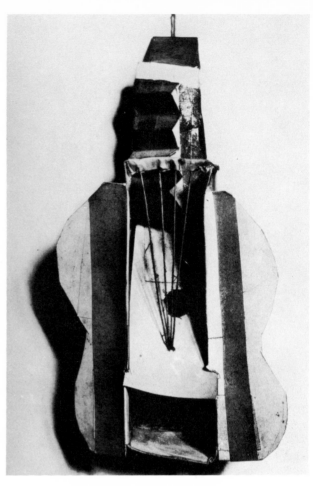

loosely be called the Hildebrand perspective. That is to say, it rejected the intellectualist notion of the sculpture as a datum of perception that calls out to be reconstituted in its entirety and that depends on the relief plane as a medium for this act of imagination.

It has become a commonplace of contemporary criticism that Cubist constructions made literal the relationships that had been only apparent in Cubist collage. "Sometime in 1912," Clement Greenberg writes, "Picasso cut out and folded a piece of paper in the shape of a guitar; to this he glued and fitted other pieces of paper and four taut strings, thus creating a sequence of flat surfaces in real and sculptural space to which there clung only the vestige of a picture plane. The affixed elements of collage were extruded, as it were, and cut off from the literal pictorial surface to form a bas-relief."[17] If we look closely at the four-year development of this enterprise, we find that the evolution we would expect—a progression from simple relief to the establishment of an increasingly independent object—is the reverse of what really happened. Instead of moving toward greater possession of three-dimensional space through a more discretely felt object, Picasso seems to have worked backward.

In 1912 he did indeed cut out the shape of a guitar, freeing it from the surface of the picture and addressing himself to it as an autonomous sculptural object (Fig. 18). But in the succeeding three years of work with these constructions, Picasso submerged the object ever more insistently into the flat or creased stretches of a convoluted relief plane. More and more he sought to reintegrate the object into the pictorial milieu, to deny the wholeness or completeness of its shape taken as an independent object. Indeed, two years later, in the constructions of 1914 (Figs. 19 and 138), the object's surface is once again coextensive with the surface of the relief. This surface does not take the shape of the object—it is not guitar- or bottle-shaped—but is insistently rectilinear and is organized along the lines of a Cubist picture. Like a painting from the years of Analytic Cubism, it seems densest at its center, while at its edges the characteristic compression of angled planes and shallow pockets of space, grouped along

[17] Greenberg, *Art and Culture*, p. 79.

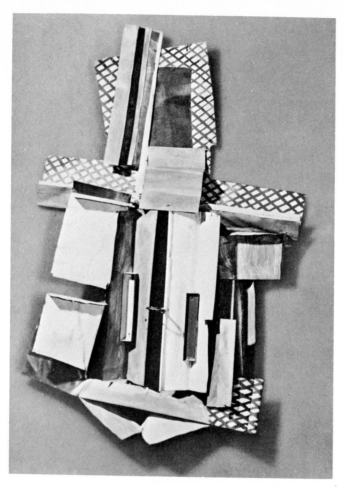

the central axes, seems to thin out into a vaguer, more traditional sense of atmosphere. The subjects of the construction are given in the positive folds and recesses at the center of the work. The contours of the objects have to be assumed as the edges of the shadows cast by folds of paper or as the negative areas left by positive cardboard shapes whose nonfigurative quality makes them seem substantiated shadow.

The reintegration of the constructed objects of 1914 into the surface of the picture raises questions about the way Picasso viewed the guitars of 1912. Why did his subsequent constructed sculptures deny those innocent, full-bodied, and unequivocal objects of the first constructions?

Picasso's first constructed guitar is fashioned like an oblong box with its top split down the center and folded out on either side (Fig. 18). These two "flaps" are cut to specify a guitar's profile. The object has a surface (the two shaped flaps) and an inside (the cavity of the box's interior). The inside is not totally open to view but half-filled; out of its depths a plane bridges the distance from the unseen and unseeable inside of the guitar to its exterior. Beginning at the upper edge of the box, the "four taut strings" of Greenberg's description converge at a point just over halfway down the face of the instrument, defying the arrangement of real strings on a real guitar. In the context of the constructions, the meaning of this convergence is entirely clear. It is an illusionistic device, lifted from a pictorial setting and transplanted into the sculpture: it reads as a perspective convention, as parallel strings seen in depth.

In this early construction, as he also did in subsequent works, Picasso abstracts depth as a convention of sight and presents it along with the physical presence of the guitar, investing the instrument with the emotional release attached to deep space but investing it gratuitously. It is as though he were saying that the physical object presents itself to the viewer in all its wholeness *as surface only* and that depth in this case is a quality that can be added to the object exactly as color can be added to it. Because of the equivocal and conventionalized presence Picasso gives it in this object, depth can speak for the first time of the possibility of its absence. Because deep space, the space that connects sight to its objects, appears here as something that is not necessarily guaranteed in sculpture, it is for the first time felt as superfluous. It as as though the space of the object were dispensible, as though it were merely the derelict remnant of an overweening naturalism.

However, the 1912 *Guitar* poses a problem that the succeeding works try to resolve. The problem does not lie in the confusion between physical presence and pictorial convention; this ambiguity is deliberate and is retained as the express meaning of all the constructions. It is the overall structure of the 1912 *Guitar* that appears problematic. Since the work takes the form of a box, it invites the viewer to read the sculptural array of shapes as projections from an unseen and mysterious core. It is as though the simple three-dimensional form of the guitar's body had been split, so that its exterior skin could be parted and held aside to reveal its masked interior. In this sense, the 1912 *Guitar* attaches itself to Boccioni's *Bottle* and the Hildebrand perspective. By alluding to the problem of empirical knowledge, it attaches itself to the central theme of the sculpture that grew up around Cubism, but that was never, properly speaking, Picasso's own. The silhouette of the guitar, in its very completeness, suggests that the instrument has some kind of a priori reality as an object of thought. As long as the guitar's structure is seen as preexistent, as a whole to be broken down by analysis, the inside-outside question continues to haunt it. Hypothetically, Picasso's objection to this work was that it seemed to locate its *raison d'être*—and, by implication, that of sculpture in general—in the effort to acquire knowledge about physical objects.

In the succeeding constructions, Picasso disallowed the shape of the objects he fashioned and submerged them into the two-dimensional context of the relief plane. He worked with them as things known only to, because through, sight, and not the "real" or "essential" constructs of late Cubism or of Futurism. In this way objects became exactly and totally comprised of the "cheat" of vision. That is to say, they became all surface, nothing but surface. If "I see the bottle or the guitar" meant only "I see the front surface of the bottle or the guitar," then the constructions of 1914 give the object in the form of that contingency that is sight itself—a contingency that Picasso progressively heightened and exacerbated through the folds and crosshatchings, the negative shapes and embodied voids that were for him the very stuff of vision resigned to surface.

Basically, what distinguished Picasso's reliefs from Rosso's or Hildebrand's was that Picasso approached sculpture with a conception of the picture plane that was modernist, while the earlier sculptors' was not. For them, the picture plane and, consequently, the relief ground were transparent, opening onto an extension of the viewer's space. For Picasso this conflictless reporting about the world was impossible. As a modernist artist, Picasso felt obliged to insist on the viewer's recognition that he was confronting an artificial object. Therefore a sense of the flat and opaque plane was made to qualify every other experience the painting might offer. When Picasso began to deal with sculpture, he transferred this attitude toward surface to the ground of the relief. In 1916 this essentially modernist conviction set Picasso apart from contemporaries like Lipchitz or Pevsner.

But when Picasso returned to sculpture in the 1930s, after a twelve-year absence from the problem, he began to allow himself the structural luxury of a core. His 1930 *Figurine* (Fig. 20) is explicitly vertebral, while his 1939 *Head of a Woman* (Fig. 21), like the Gonzalez *Head,* arranges linear profiles and disclike planes to circumscribe the original mass of the solid object, beyond which the viewer is given access to the "real" structure. The wit and insouciance of Picasso's elaboration of this structural formula is characteristic of his later style. The two colanders of the head, seamed into a perforated sphere behind the plane of the face, infuse the totemlike assemblage with the deadpan domesticity of a French provincial kitchen. This joining of the exotic with the ordinary makes even more pointed Picasso's use of the spherical shell as a reference to the object's center of being, secreted within the artifacts of everyday life.

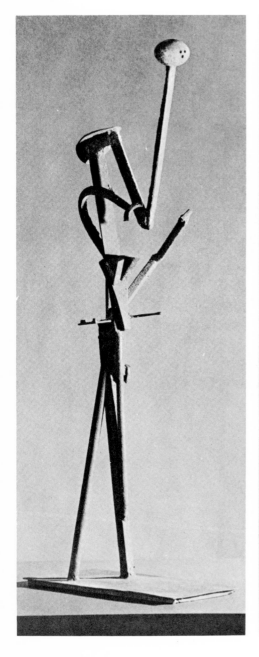

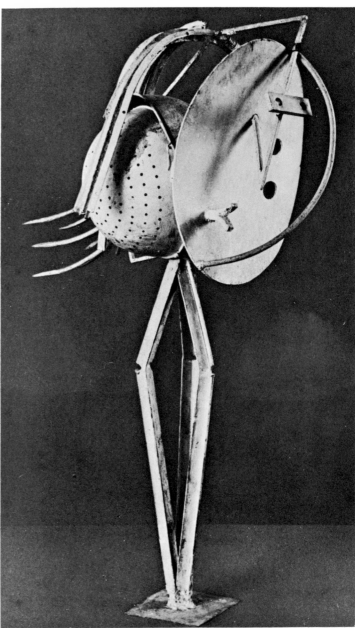

20
Picasso. *Figurine*.
1930–1932. Iron, 32½
× 10½ × 12¾ inches.
Collection of the
artist.
21
Picasso. *Head of a
Woman*. 1931. Iron,
painted white, 40 ×
14¾ × 24½ inches.
Collection of the
artist.

The Surface
of Objects

The striking originality of Smith's first welded sculpture, executed in the early thirties,
arises from its radical criticism of the European constructors' implicit adherence to the
old notions of the closed sculptural volume. In his first ventures into a three-dimensional
medium, Smith did not think of himself as a "sculptor"[18] and therefore did not bring to
bear the preconceptions about craft and the need to reveal the essence of the object
that clouded most discussion of sculpture at that time.[19] Perhaps because he did not

[18] In a curious letter written in 1956 John Graham, David Smith thanked the older painter for
having convinced him in the late spring of 1935 to become a sculptor: "Remember May 1935 when
we walked down 57th St. after your show at Garland Gallery, how you influenced me to concentrate on sculpture. I'm of course forever glad that you did, it's more my energy, though I make 200
color drawings a year. . . . But I paint or draw as a sculptor, I have no split identity as I did in 1935.
Forever thanks." Smith had begun to sculpt in 1932 and to weld in 1933. Yet, as the letter to Graham
shows, in his first ventures into a three-dimensional medium, Smith did not consider himself a
sculptor.

[19] In 1932, when Wilenski wrote *The Meaning of Modern Sculpture*, he defined the medium as "the
art of fashioning objects with three-dimensional meaning." As Wilenski explained it, this meaning
was essentialist in character and had to do with "the meaning of [the] geometrical forms" that lay
behind brute appearances. As an illustration he recalled Ruskin, in his 1870 lecture at Oxford, holding
up a crystal sphere as the essential type of sculptural form. (R. L. Wilenski, *The Meaning of Modern
Sculpture* [London: Faber and Faber, 1932], pp. 86–88.) Carola Giedion-Welcker also wrote that the
simplification of form into primal or essential volumes was behind all advanced sculptural effort.
She went on to explain that this might not necessarily entail a sculpture of mass but, as in the
example of Gabo, might lead to the creation of "virtual volumes." (*Modern Plastic Art* [Zurich: H.
Girsberger, 1937], p. 15.) However, in this country the search for essential forms was synonymous
with "this search for the essence of life bound up in the material . . ." (Andrew Ritchie, *Sculpture
of the Twentieth Century* [New York: Museum of Modern Art, 1953], p. 23) or an aesthetic of
direct carving. In Wilenski's words, direct carving involved a "collaboration between the sculptor
and the substance," so that the essence of the material and the essence of the form would be
coextensive. The authority of the carve-direct ideology had to do in part with the preeminent reputation of Maillol, and in part with the vogue for primitive sculpture. In the 1930s, in this country,
both the art magazines and the exhibitions of advanced sculpture were devoted to carve-direct
examples. If one looks through the catalogues of the Whitney Annuals, for instance, one sees the
way in which so-called progressive sculpture was consistently represented by names like Chaim
Gross, Zorach, Robus, Flanagan, Nakian, and Lachaise, to name only a few. Much of the truculence
of Smith's public pronouncements arose from his need to challenge the dogma of this aesthetic.
Thus he wrote: "I do not accept the monolithic limit in the tradition of sculpture" (IV/386) and
"I have spoken against tradition, but only the tradition of others who would hold art from moving
forward" (IV/1005).

identify himself as a sculptor, Smith was able, in the works of the early 1930s, to refrain from demanding of himself a definition of sculpture. No matter how indebted Smith was to Picasso and Gonzalez for the idea of using welded metal as a sculptural medium, and no matter how many details he imported from their works, which he saw reproduced in the *Cahiers d'art,* Smith held himself aloof from the basic preoccupations of these men. While he clearly involved himself in the themes of Giacometti's work from the early 1930s,[20] he did not allow this borrowed imagery of encaged or pinioned, helpless flesh to usurp the place of his own quite different formal content. Smith's *Suspended Figure* of 1935 (Fig. 22) rejects the central spine of Giacometti's *Woman with Her Throat Cut* (Fig. 23) or Gonzalez's *Head* and instead projects the figure in terms of a shifting and elusive exterior shell. His 1936 *Aerial Construction* is also completely vacant at its center, so that its linear patterns cannot read as the contours of a transparent but nonetheless present monolith. Rather, they must relate to surfaces that are somehow disconnected, disjunctive, and shifting relative to one another because no core, not even a relief plane, will grant them a fixed point of unity.

It was in this insistence on surface disconnected from an underlying structure that Smith's initial insight lay. This disjunction promoted his and the viewer's anxiety over the fluctuating, elusive quality of appearances. For Smith, the sculptural object had to declare its unlikeness to physical objects in general. It had to be seen as simultaneously like and unlike all other inert objects, so that its sphere of meaning could be withdrawn from the world of empirical investigation and redirected toward another, quite different world. This simultaneity has much in common with the way illusion in painting

[20] The depiction of a recumbent female figure persists within Smith's work from 1935 until about 1955, with an occasional reprise in the late fifties and sixties. He was most completely involved with the theme during the late 1930s, when according to his own accounts (e.g., "Notes on My Work," *Arts* 34 [February 1960]: 44), he was scanning *Cahiers d'art* for information about advanced sculpture in Europe. The issues of *Cahiers d'art* that were in Smith's library at the time of his death are: no. 8 (1926); no. 10 (1929); nos. 1, 4, 5, and 6 (1930); nos. 6, 7, and the "Picasso: 1930–35" issue (1936); nos. 1, 2, 3, 4, and 5 (1937); and nos. 1, 2, 3, and 4 (1939). Many of his variations on the theme recall works by Giacometti reproduced in *Cahiers d'art,* nos. 8, 9, and 10 (1932), pp. 337 ff.

22
Suspended Figure.
1935. Iron, 21¾ × 27½
× 10¼ inches. Estate
of the artist.
23
Alberto Giacometti.
*Woman with Her
Throat Cut.* 1932.
Bronze, 34½ inches.
Museum of Modern
Art, New York.

locates meaning in the tension between the clues to depth a painting offers and its actual flatness.

In his early sculpture, Smith drew this kind of illusionism from the absence of an organizing spine, which implied the absence of a graspable object as well. By the time, late in his career, when he had done *Zig IV*, Smith could offer his illusionism in terms of a present object, although of a very special kind. In this sense *Zig IV* climaxes Smith's experience in the 1950s, when he had discovered the fruitfulness of directing all the elements in his work toward forcing an analogy between the surface of a sculpture and the planar surface of a painting.[21] Smith had early been initiated into Cubism's subversion of drawing and shading, which converted the normal agents of illusionism into the means of achieving a direct experience of the painting surface itself, in all its flatness, wholeness, and openness to view. By the late fifties and early sixties, Smith understood the imperatives for grafting onto sculpture the kind of surface that derived from Cubism's acknowledgment of the picture plane in modernist art. The picture's actual surface, unlike that of a three-dimensional object, is one that can be seen completely. By making sculpture that would be perceived in terms of extended and interconnected surfaces, Smith could force the viewer to recognize that the sculpture spread before him was unlike other objects. To force the work to appear entirely open and *visible* from a fixed point of view is to provoke the illusion that a sculptural object, like a picture surface, can be known all at once. The knowledge it addresses itself to is knowledge of this fact rather than any "essentialist" knowledge about the physical world, because when surface becomes that thing beyond which there is nothing to see, then the sculpture is wholly unlike objects in the world.

Up to this point, I have been presenting Smith's work as though between parentheses. At one end of his career his early sculpture turns its back on the formal premise of

[21] This notion of surface as a medium of sculpture was first discussed by Michael Fried, in reference, to a work by Jules Olitski. ("Art and Objecthood," *Artforum* 5 [Summer 1967]: 21.) I am in his debt for this idea, which is, in my view, essential to understanding the later Smith. Other articles of his have also helped to shape my understanding of sculpture, among which I would like particularly to acknowledge the essay on Stella.

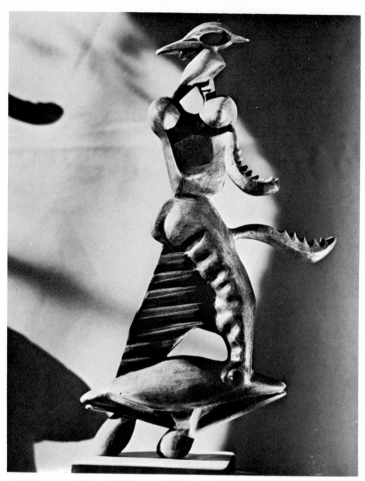

24
*Reclining Con-
struction.* 1936.
Iron, 14 × 26⅞ × 6⅛
inches. Estate of the
artist.
25
Reclining Figure.
1953. Steel, 25½ ×
13½ × 3½ inches.
Estate of the artist.

26
Aftermath Figure.
1945. Bronze, 13⅜ ×
7⅝ × 3 inches.
Estate of the artist.

what is normally thought of as advanced sculpture. At the other end, *Zig IV* unfolds what seems to be an authoritative solution to the problems of an entire artistic lifetime. Between that beginning and that end lies the product of thirty years of labor.

So far I have said nothing explicit about those three decades or their contents. However, all of the preceding discussion has assumed that it makes sense to juxtapose the early and late work, even though it results in separating the career from its historical background and fashioning the material according to a particular pattern, in this instance one of initial problem and successive solutions. The implication is that the beginning and the end of Smith's career were related not just chronologically, but logically. In other words, I have been assuming that a single issue guided the development of Smith's style, a single question overarched thirty years of labor, shaping in its own image all of Smith's reactions to the changing face of European and American art.

While it does not seem particularly controversial to make this kind of assumption about the work of, say, Cézanne or Matisse, artists whose careers strike one as particularly insular and reflexive, it might indeed appear to be an unwarranted assumption to make about David Smith. More than almost any other American's, Smith's work has always been viewed by historians and critics as having fed continuously on the substance of advanced European art.[22] As one ideology or style supplanted the other in Paris—Cubism giving way to Constructivism, both of them yielding place to Surrealism— and as these new directions spread through the art world at large, Smith responded by changing his own course. His maturity (like that of postwar American art in general) is accordingly seen as the product of a succession of influences, or to make room for the magnitude of his originality, the inspired amalgam of the fundamental ideas of the three major twentieth-century styles.

[22] Kramer writes, "In effect [Smith] restored the Constructivist idea to the Cubist tradition which had spawned it in the first place and then threw in the Surrealism of his generation for good measure. Once this synthesis was achieved, Smith moved freely in and out of figurative and nonfigurative modes; heads, figures, landscapes, animal images, mythical and Surrealist fantasies, the symbolic anecdote and the purely formalistic conception were all available to his medium." ("David Smith," *Arts* 34 [February 1960]: 31.) Nine years later another critic writing on Smith presented exactly the same picture. See Sheldon Nodelman, "David Smith," *Art News* 68 (February 1969): 56.

27
Oculus. 1947.
Steel, 37 × 32½ × 10
inches. Collection
Robert E. John, New
York.
28
House in Landscape.
1945. Steel, 18½ ×
24¾ × 6 inches. Col-
lection George Irwin,
Quincy, Illinois.

However, to concentrate on Smith's development with a historical formula in mind creates a disturbing dissonance. For within any one period of his activity, there is much that must appear anomalous if this or that putative influence is accepted. Smith consistently produced contemporaneous ranges of sculpture whose formal impulses are not just highly diverse but mutually exclusive. Thus, we might consider the appearance during the 1940s of small, compact, smoothly modeled statuettes, which conjure with the spectral imagery of Ernst's *Hordes* or the nightmare population of Tanguy's landscapes, as evidence of Smith's Surrealist convictions. But then we would also be tempted to explain as Surrealist-inspired the simultaneous appearance in other works of a linearly wrought framework and a vocabulary of found objects. The Surrealist explanation seems itself to need explaining. For surely Smith *meant* two different things by these two different groups of objects—the solid statuettes and the weblike landscapes—and surely we still are in no position to understand why he dropped one track of work and continued the other.

Similar problems arise if we try to explain the production of the 1950s by means of the supposed sharing of concerns with the Abstract-Expressionist painters. For while it might encourage the notion that Smith's breakthrough into modernism was a rejection of the human figure, it fails to explain the best works Smith made during these years. It is true that in 1951 Smith made sculptures like *Hudson River Landscape* (Fig. 60) and *The Banquet* (Fig. 29), sculptures of landscape in which a pictorial expanse of metal line breaks off all reference to the human body. But it is equally true that the great sculpture of the 1950s, the *Agricolas*, the *Tanktotems*, and the *Sentinels*, are all upright, evoking the form of the human body, although certainly not its density or volume. The great Smiths of the fifties have nothing to do with landscape. Instead, they almost compulsively repeat the same basic configuration: a planar, frontal torso; a laconic head; a tripodlike connection with the ground. The persistence of this image through the fifties and sixties to the great final series of Smith's career—the *Cubis*—seems to call for an explanation. If the explanation by recourse to the evolution of twentieth-century style does not serve, neither does reference to Smith's own pub-

29
The Banquet. 1951.
Steel, 53⅛ × 80¾ ×
13½ inches. Private
collection.

lished statements. Perhaps the most garrulous of all the postwar American artists, Smith's archive is filled with lectures, declarations, definitions, exhortations. But these are curiously uninformative, and often appear to have been a kind of evasion.[23]

Yet Smith did leave behind something like a key to his meaning. In the sculpture itself, he left the traces of a private dialogue that was carried on in the form of a narrowly repetitive set of images. In a certain sense, these images were the tiger riding the back of Smith's sculpture. They are the one feature of his work that seems to relate both to his most personal experience and to his most openly expressed formal convictions. For that reason I have judged the isolation and interpretation of that imagery to be the most reliable way to begin an overall characterization of Smith's art.

[23] See Chapter 2, pp. 51–55.

30
Tanktotem IV. (on left)
1953. Steel, 92½ ×
33½ × 29 inches.
Albright-Knox Gallery,
Buffalo.
Tanktotem III. (on right)
1953. Steel, 84½ ×
27 × 20 inches. Estate
of the artist.

31
Tanktotem V. 1955–
1956. Steel, 96¾ ×
52 inches. Collection
Howard and Jean
Lipman, Cannondale,
Connecticut.

32
Sentinel IV. 1957.
Steel, painted black,
80 × 29 × 32 inches.
Private collection.

33
Voltri XIII. 1962. Steel,
64⅛ × 103¾ inches.
Estate of the artist.

Chapter Two

Smith's Imagery: The Cannon, the Totem, the Sacrifice

Imagery in the Early Work

Landscapes of the Fifties

The Totem

With *Zig IV* one can begin to assess Smith's achievement. An example of Smith's mature style, *Zig IV* makes manifest both a new visual idea and a new way of arresting the viewer, making him stop and examine, as though for the first time, his own relationship to objects. *Zig IV* is exemplary, but any one of a dozen monumental pieces in the astonishingly full repertory of Smith's work in the 1960s would show the same formal intelligence in operation. The rate at which he was able to strike off great sculptures, the fecundity of his ideas, the apparent ease with which one masterful piece followed another, all of this is part of the phenomenon of David Smith's mature career. It was also the basis for the legends that grew up around him as a "personality" in later years. These were structures of myth that he himself often helped create,[1] for shielded by them he could intransigently refuse to talk about the meaning or relative quality of any one of his sculptures.[2] An instance of this self-mythologizing comes from Smith's stay at Voltri, Italy, in 1962. There he turned out twenty-six monumental sculptures in one month and then, like an athlete who claims to be out of practice for fear of losing, shrugged off this accomplishment as the result of a "mistake." (In order to be able to gauge the prodigious size of this output, it should be noted that in 1953 Smith had written to a friend telling him that owing to the Guggenheim fellowship, which had released him from teaching, he had had a record year for sculpture: he had actually produced twenty pieces over the course of twelve months.)[3]

The applause and amazement that greeted Smith's feat at Voltri was a characteristic response to the public David Smith: "And Vulcan came to Voltri."[4] Smith's response

[1] Smith often made a point of his poverty during the thirties and forties and his consequent need to work. In his statement for Elaine de Kooning's article, "David Smith Makes a Sculpture," *Art News* 50 (September 1951): 37, he wrote: "All my life, the work day has been any part of the twenty-four, on oil tankers, driving hacks, . . . three shifts in factories." His first wife, Dorothy Dehner, has said that Smith exaggerated this aspect of his life greatly, and that due to a small income of hers at this time Smith's obligation to work at odd jobs was almost nonexistent. See *David Smith by David Smith,* ed. Cleve Gray (New York: Holt, Rinehart & Winston, 1968), p. 174, fnn. 12, 16.
[2] See Chapter 1, fn. 4.
[3] Letter to Harvard Arnason, Archive I/1210.
[4] Giovanni Carandente, *Voltron* (Philadelphia: University of Pennsylvania Press, 1964), p. 5.

was also typical. He disavowed any personal motive, claiming instead that, not understanding Italian, he had not realized that he was expected to create only one or at the
most two works for the exhibition at Spoleto (to which he was to contribute at the
end of his residence at the factory-workshop provided at Voltri). Smith's "mistake" is a
characteristic subterfuge,[5] a curtain dropped between himself and the pyrotechnical
display he mounted at Voltri, a display whose climax was to have been the triumphal
entrance into Spoleto of a mammoth sculpture with a railroad car for its base. That
huge sculpture, hurtling into the medieval city already decorated with works by Henry
Moore, Chadwick, and Calder, would have been like the final, wanton gesture of a
challenger at a potlatch ceremony, who, knowing he will win, flings a matchless
treasure into the sea. Because the railroad tunnels along the west coast of Italy were
too low to accommodate the projected work, the flatcar sculpture was never built,
but Smith later wrote:

A dream is a dream never lost. . . . I found an old flat car asked for and was given it—
Had I used the flatcar for the base and made a sculpture on the top the dream would
have been closer. . . . I could have made a car with the nude bodies of machines,
undressed of their detail and teeth. . . . In a year I could have made a train.[6]

 Just as he temporized over the reasons for his achievement at Voltri, Smith refused to
analyze any part of his development, repeating instead variations on the formula
quoted at the beginning of these pages. He consigned the enormous emotional cost
of his work into some deep subterranean preserve, permitting the outsider to focus
only on those affectless formal distinctions that he claimed he was able to make at

[5] While in Italy, Smith was provided with an interpreter by Italsider, the national steel company,
which had also arranged for him to use its abandoned factories at Voltri as a studio. If the interpreter
was not able to clarify the nature of the sculptural commission, then surely the sculptor Lynn Chadwick would have. Chadwick, who lived in the same hotel in Genoa as Smith did, was also working
under Italsider's patronage for the festival at Spoleto and fully understood the extent of the commission. In Italy Smith and Chadwick became "good friends—prowled night life Genoa together"
(ibid., p. 11) and surely must have discussed not only their ongoing work but the very unusual commission that had prompted it.
[6] Written in 1962, either at Voltri or upon Smith's return to Bolton Landing. Archive IV/708.

36
Zig IV. (side view)
(See Figs. 6 and 7.)

the very outset of his sculptural career. Nevertheless, as one surveys Smith's achievement, it is obvious that it was nurtured by the very emotions he refused to acknowledge. If there is reason to examine the content of the sculpture, it is to see how and at what level Smith's formal convictions intersected with private sources of feeling. It is to understand how his own anxieties and desires heightened and at the same time modified his response to the conceptual implications of the sculpture produced in Europe during the first half of this century.

In order to trace the content of Smith's mature style back through the labyrinth of his development, I shall summarize what has been formulated so far about *Zig IV:* (1) it eludes possession insofar as it cannot be mastered in terms of tactile experience, nor understood through an a priori intellectual concept; (2) it can be possessed completely by vision alone, unlike the real objects of our experience; (3) Smith's sculpture seems totally comprehensible from a single viewing point, even where it makes sense to move around the work; (4) the very availability of the surface sets into motion expectations about the availability of objects; (5) the work composes itself into an image related to the carefully guarded private feelings Smith had about his work.

This last characteristic may seem surprising, especially because we tend to think of the late sculpture in general, and the *Zigs* in particular, as being totally abstract.[7] At the level of formal investigation, the issues these later works raise are preponderantly those of abstract sculpture, for Smith's personal and obsessive emotions had been transmuted into formal concerns by the middle 1950s. However, *Zig IV* can be read at quite another level: with its mortarlike tubular segments poised on its tilted platform, like a partially dismantled antiaircraft gun, the sculpture makes (like *Zigs VII* and *VIII*) an elliptical reference to a cannon.

[7] Greenberg has said of *Zig IV* that "in it he escapes entirely from the allusions to the natural world (which includes man) that abound elsewhere in his art. Abstract form—with perhaps some reference to urban landscape—guides the eye exclusively here." See "David Smith," *Art in America* 54 (January 1966): 28.

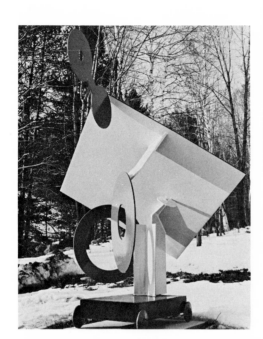

37a
Zig. VII. 1963. Steel,
painted cream, red,
and blue, 94¾ × 100⅜
inches. Estate of the
artist.
37b
Zig VIII. 1964. Steel,
painted red, black,
and white, 100⅜ ×
87½ inches. Museum
of Fine Arts, Boston.
38
Zig VII and *Zig VIII.*
(alternate views)

39
War Landscape.
1947. Bronze, 9 × 7
× 6 inches. Estate of
the artist.

The single factor that emerges from a survey of Smith's work is the recurrence of a group of four images, of which the cannon is a central member. The obsessiveness with which he returned to these images again and again, as though to a task he could not finish, suggests that, rather than serving as the pretext for his sculpture, they were the provocation. Looking at Smith's development in the 1940s with this imagery in mind reveals: first, a mode of working that allowed Smith to talk about issues that really concerned him, but only at the price of suppressing his own "voice"; second, the emergence late in the decade of a more original formal language that, because it evoked landscape, ended by addressing nothing that concerned him, nothing he found meaningful; and finally, as I shall show, the reconciliation of these opposing strains in the conceptual structure of the totem.

Imagery in
the Early Work

Zig IV was not the first cannon to appear in Smith's production. The *Medals for Dishonor* that preoccupied Smith from 1938 to 1940 abound with cannon, both in the preparatory drawings and in their finished state. We would expect Smith to refer to these weapons as agents of violence and destruction in the fervently antimilitarist polemic of these medals,[8] but the specific image Smith chose to suggest the brutality of war was that of a cannon as a violator of women. It is this particular image of physical contact between the cannon and the female figure, with its combination of violence and sexuality, that returns again and again over the succeeding two decades.

Smith carried the association between the violence of the cannon and sexual violation into his subsequent work on two levels. The first relates to the physical form of the cannon, its phallic character, which Smith emphasized in his sketchbooks and incorporated into almost every large-scale work of the 1940s. In drawings and sculptures that show the cannon with wings (and often with small vestigial legs), Smith specified the sexual character of the cannon (see Figs. 39, 40, and 54) both in the graphic detail he

[8] In his autobiography Smith explained the origins of the *Medals:* "From 1936 after I came back from Europe I was impressed by Sumerian Seals—Intaglio concept in general—a collection of [German] war medals I had seen in the British Museum. I decided to do a series of Anti-war Medallions called Medals for Dishonor." See Archive IV/275.

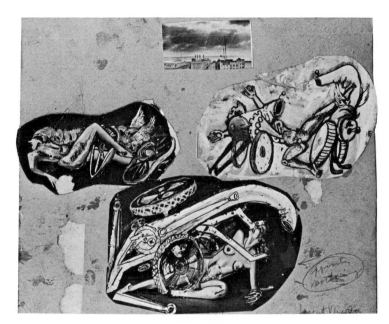

40
Uncatalogued page in
the Archive. Early
1940s.
41
Uncatalogued page in
the Archive. Early
1940s.

42
Page from Sketch-
book #41. 1944–1954.
Archive IV/58.
43
Pieter Breughel. Detail
from *Sloth*. 1557. One
of a series of engrav-
ings of *The Seven
Deadly Sins.*

used and by making it resemble the winged phallus of classical antiquity.[9] An added characteristic of the cannon drawings is that Smith usually showed them to be hollow shells that contained animal or human grotesques.[10] He seems to have conceived them as masks that could be put on and cast aside at will.[11]

The person who was most strongly linked with the role suggested by the cannon was Smith himself. In a 1947 speech, he said, "In psychoanalytic terms we speak of a shift of narcissistic cathexis from the person of the artist to his work,"[12] and somewhat later

[9] Smith probably discovered the winged phallus that was represented in countless classical bronzes either when he was in Greece in 1936 or during his visits to the British Museum. After the *Medals for Dishonor* were finished, Emile, the man who had cast them, presented Smith with a silver winged phallus in memory of their collaboration. Told to the author by Dorothy Dehner.

[10] Reel V in the Archive includes a collection of Smith's source material. In addition to other items relevant to Smith's work of the late thirties (for example, a Schongauer print of Leda and the swan and several impressions made by Sumerian seals), there is a sequence of reproductions of Breughel engravings illustrating the seven deadly sins. The engraving of *Sloth* is particularly relevant to the development of the hollow, animated cannon/phallus, for the fantastic creature at its lower left is a hollow fish with legs, out of which peers the face of a man. Smith later wrote of his 1950 sculpture *The Fish,* that it was "the first fish who was a man." (*David Smith* [Marion Willard Gallery, New York, March–April, 1951]). Two drawings from the early 1940s developing the idea of the hollow, erotic shell that could be filled and animated by an actor are IV/32 and IV/51. (See Figs. 44 and 54.) The drawings Smith was making at this time and some of the sketches he made throughout his life (see Figs. 40, 46, and 47) relate to fantasies of oral and anal eroticism. Along with the recurrent characterization of the phallus as hollow, they reveal the fear of impotence that obsessed him throughout his adult life. Conversation with Jean Smith.

[11] The masklike character is clear in Drawing IV/51 (Fig. 44) and in a drawing of the later 1940s (Fig. 48) showing a turtle wearing a mask in the form of a brutish human head. Under this Smith had written: "Turtles are vertebrae forming housing, the human form housed, the growth of the Great Order of vertebrae," and "the world still belongs to the reptiles, the jurassic cretaceous." (Under this note is a reference to Marcel Prenant's *Biology and Marxism.*) While animals are the symbols for predatory human behavior in the 1945 sculptures of the spectres, Smith represented this kind of atavism in his sketchbooks by means of masks. The earliest appearance in Smith's work of creatures wearing masks is found in the *Medal for Dishonor: Death by Gas.* In his notes to the *Medals,* Smith speaks of "the foetus who, from environment, will be born masked"; he seems to have been pointing to the idea that survival is possible only to those who assume the characteristics of the agents of brutality.

[12] From a speech given at Skidmore College on February 17, 1947. See Archive IV/743.

45
One of the two fields at Bolton Landing in which Smith set out his sculpture.

he was to say of a sculpture, "I've made it because it comes closer to saying who I am than any other method I can use. The work is my identity."[13] Smith always spoke of his sculpture as the only thing that guaranteed him an identity, that without his role as a sculptor he would have no identity. For him, identity seems in fact to have been tied to things he produced[14] and to the surface characteristics of his own person.[15] It is paradoxical that beginning in 1942 Smith took evident satisfaction in helping to produce army tanks, the very instruments of destruction that he had earlier found so abhorrent.[16]

[13] From a speech at Ohio State University, April 17, 1959. See Archive IV/1009. Similar statements were: "The sculpture-work is a statement of my identity" (*Everyday Art Quarterly*, no. 23 [Winter 1952], p. 21), and "Art is made from the inside of who you are when you face yourself" (speech given at the August 1954 Woodstock Conference).

[14] In 1956, when Smith left his longtime dealer, Marion Willard, he explained that he did not like his sculptures to be away from him, whether in storage in New York or traveling in exhibitions; that he wanted them near him all the time, planted in his fields. (See Archive, Reel II.) He seems to have felt that only physical possession of his offspring could assure him of who he was. In 1961 Gordon Washburn, the director of the Carnegie Institute of Art, wrote to Smith asking him to lower the prices on the sculptures that were being exhibited at the time of the Pittsburgh International. Mr. Washburn advised Smith that his prices were higher than Picasso's. Smith wrote back immediately offering to remove his sculpture from the exhibition. His truculence in this matter recalls his behavior with Marion Willard, and in a letter in 1961 (see Reel II) Smith reiterated his desire to keep his sculptures around him in the fields at Bolton Landing. This possessiveness extended to his real children as well, for at the time of his second divorce he threatened to leave the country to avoid paying for their support unless he could have them near him. (See Motherwell Reel of Archive.)

[15] In 1942, when his co-workers in a Schenectady plant (which produced equipment for the U.S. Army) pinned him to the ground and shaved off his beard, Smith was enraged because he felt he had been stripped of his identity. This was related to the author in conversation with Dorothy Dehner.

[16] In the three years in Schenectady, during which he worked eight hours a day in the factory as a welder on M7 tanks and locomotives, Smith identified himself increasingly with his fellow workers. Not only was he fiercely proud of his status within the factory unit as a "first class armor plate welder" (see Archive IV/280), but his sculptural output dropped off radically at this time, as he became absorbed by his work in the munitions plant. From 1942 to 1944 he made almost no metal sculpture, beginning instead to learn stonecutting and carving, and in the entire span of those three years he produced only fifteen pieces. Of course Smith's job consumed much of his time, leaving little available for sculpture during these years. Even so, the rate of five pieces a year for an artist whose career was already ten years old is surprisingly small.

46
Untitled etching. 1942.
Estate of the artist.
47
Untitled etching. 1942.
Estate of the artist.
48
Page from Notebook
#27. Mid-1940s.
Archive III/997.

These conflicting attitudes of revulsion and pride toward the connotations of the cannon have their analogue in the contradictory positions Smith took toward steel itself. For the second connotation that the cannon seems to have carried was that its very material—Smith's chosen medium—was inextricably bound to the idea of brutality. "Possibly steel is so beautiful," Smith wrote, "because of all the movement associated with it, its strength and functions. . . . Yet it is also brutal: the rapist, the murderer and death-dealing giants are also its offspring."[17] And he would add, "The iron element I hold in high respect."[18] While he thus seems to have revered the material he worked with and to have prized its invulnerability, he had conflicting feelings about it. For steel is *not* invulnerable to deterioration, and Smith found himself relishing the idea of the perishable, mutable qualities of this seemingly indestructible substance: "I am slightly pleased when I see rust on stainless material, the soft acid stain which denotes either contamination of iron from the grinding wheel or lack of balance in the alloy, or possibly it states philosophically that the stainless is not wholly pure and has a susceptibility as do humans, to the stain of avowed purpose to the actual."[19]

In contrast to sculptors like Arp and Moore, with their camp-meeting religiosity about stone, wood, and the essential forms lying nascent within their materials, Smith's respect for steel, the honor he paid it as a substance, was countered by an attitude toward it that was almost vengeful. Unlike the direct carvers, who released the sculptural object like surgeons assisting a birth, for Smith the very act of making a sculpture had to be an act of destruction. Arc welding causes the separate pieces to melt and run together; torch cutting punctures and burns the metal. The direct carvers wanted the product of their labor to be relished through the beholder's recapitulation of its creation. Their dogmas defined sculpture as a medium that was essentially tactile, meant to be handled and to be possessed. Smith seems to have been horrified by the prospect of a viewer's reenacting his own creative process. Asked in an interview if he liked people

[17] Quoted in Elaine de Kooning, "David Smith Makes a Sculpture."
[18] From a speech given at the Museum of Modern Art, February 21, 1952. See Archive III/1338 and IV/360.
[19] See Archive IV/18.

to touch his work, he responded: "I think sculpture along with any art is strictly a visual response . . . the touch for me was a matter of physical labor on my part, and I don't touch, I touch with the eye."[20] Even if the physical labor involved in the fabrication of steel sculpture violates the material, the form of the finished sculpture can become a monumental prohibition against touching it. As in the case of *Zig IV*, it was the immunization of the sculpture against the viewer's grasp or his desire to possess that opened up for Smith vast reaches of untrodden formal territory.

In this case, as in so many others, Smith's formal ideas are consistent with, if not actually directed by, less controlled emotional reflexes. Steel is potentially dangerous ("death-dealing giants are its offspring"), and therefore one must not touch it, but it is also vulnerable and must itself be protected from being touched. Whether Smith identified its potential as that of violator or violated or both, he seems to have been determined to insulate the steel sculpture within a set of restrictive sanctions. Thus, if the tripartite association between cannon and phallus and steel is important, it is because it is the basis for an emotional equation that Smith finally solved in formal terms. The left-hand side of the equation had to do with fantasies (and fears) of brutalizing objects, both human objects and the sculptural objects that were their surrogates. The right-hand side became a formal interdiction, prohibiting contact. Once the prohibition or taboo has reached the level of a coherent formal language, it has become public. Its directives and the conventions within which they are legible are open to any viewer of the sculptures. But the prohibition seems to have begun as a private interdiction, in order to establish a rigid, almost ritualistic boundary between the sculpture Smith made and the violence that was continually seething within him.

The violence that Smith directed toward the people who were closest to him had always been his characteristic reaction to stress. As a child, he had set off dynamite in the fields around Decatur, and in high school he had loaded and fired the town's Civil War cannon. Although he was constantly being told to stay away from them, he hopped freight trains and ran on the moving boxcars. "As a kid in Indiana," he said, "the most

[20] Interview on station WNCN by Marion Honesko, October 25, 1964. (On tape in the Detroit Archives.)

49
Atrocity. 1943. Bronze,
4 × 6½ × 3¼ inches.
Collection Mr. and
Mrs. Lester Talkington,
Tappan, New York.

50
Page from Sketchbook
#23. 1933–1945.
Archive III/838.

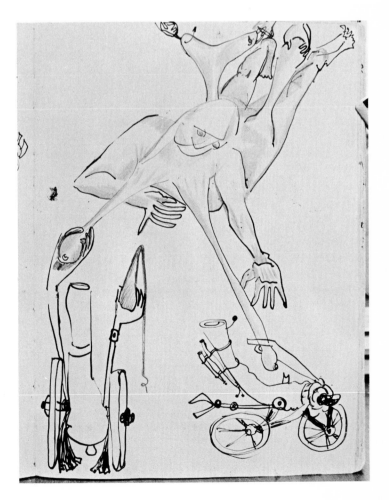

fascinating thing in the world was the railroad engine. It was also the most taboo."[21]

Over and over again in later life, talking about his career as an artist, Smith preached resistance to authority. He pictured sculpture as perpetually in need of rebelling against categories handed down by the "pretending authorities"[22] or the "verbalizers and proselytizers."[23] The violent fervor of his declarations of artistic independence seems to recall his intractable and almost frantic assertions of will as a boy. The brutality of Smith's rebellious play assumed a particularly nightmarish quality when it was turned against himself. His capacity for self-hate and self-punishment seems to have been very great. He claimed that once, after his father had whipped him and sent him to his room, he climbed down from his window and in pajamas and bare feet ran six miles through the snow to his grandmother's house.[24] There is no way of telling whether this incident is apocryphal or not; in any case, it speaks to the tremendous energy Smith could summon up to vent his rage against the intrusion of outside authority into his world.[25]

[21] Ibid.

[22] See Archive IV/488.

[23] "Art and Religion," *Art Digest* 28 (December 15, 1953): 11. Smith had also said, "In childhood we have been raped by word pictures [traditional concepts]. We must revolt against all word authority. Our only language is vision" (IV/369). Or again, he insisted, "The ogres of authority I reject. . . . I maintain the rage and develop its resource." *The Whitney Review* (New York: Whitney Museum of American Art, 1962), n.p.

[24] Related to me in conversation with Dorothy Dehner, who said that Smith's father never strapped or hit Smith as a child.

In his most important early memory, he again defeats an attempt to punish him, this time by making a work of art. He recalls that at a very young age, having been punished by being tied to a tree, he sat down and fashioned a lion out of mud. He remembers this act as being greeted with applause and admiration. Smith recounted this scene in at least two different versions. In one, he was three years old when it happened; in the other, five years old. The second version also changed the identity of the admiring parent. In the first (recounted to Garnet McCoy by Dorothy Dehner, on record in the Detroit Archives) it was his mother who exclaimed over him; in the second ("Sculpture Is," *Possibilities* 1 [1947–1948]: 25) his grandmother.

[25] As an adult, in a frenzied reaction to a reprimand by his first wife, Smith attempted suicide. (Dorothy Dehner, in conversation.)

Smith had mustered all his formal power to make an early work like *Aerial Construction* an exvertebrate object, a thing of surfaces. But with a primitive part of his being he also responded to something that was inherent in the very art he was bent on rejecting. Smith was thus simultaneously repelled by and attracted to the Surrealist drama of desire, possession, and violation being staged by the European sculpture of the midthirties. One finds evidence of this ambivalence in the small details that twist his early pieces like an iconographic tic, showing Smith's absorption in the essentially sadistic image of Giacometti's *Woman with Her Throat Cut.*[26] Throughout the 1930s Smith repeats this image of the violated female figure. In some works he gave himself up both to the form and to the content of Giacometti's object. But in many others, as I have shown, he transmuted the image into a formal mode that stated his personal and original rejection of the core and his preoccupation with surfaces.

By the end of the 1930s, Smith's fascination with violent imagery became more overt, shaping the whole sculpture rather than appearing only furtively in small details. This preoccupation with iconography seems for a time during the 1940s to have snuffed out the formal independence Smith had gained in the preceding decade. In 1939–1940 Smith cast his *Medals for Dishonor* as a traditional drama by setting solidly modeled actors into naturalistic pockets of stagelike space. Whatever stylization of the figures or dislocation of space we find in the *Medals* is both timid and derivative. It seems dependent on the kind of combination of German Expressionism and Surrealism that is offered, for example, by the work of Max Beckmann.[27]

The strange acceptance of the vocabulary of solid, volumetric forms that had begun in the *Medals* continues into the 1940s. It is behind Smith's experiments with stone carving from 1942 to 1944, and it appears in the small-scale cast bronze and fabricated

[26] Giacometti's *Woman with Her Throat Cut* clearly inspired the lolling head and helpless arms of *Reclining Construction* (1936) and the exposed vertebrae of *Suspended Figure* (1935); just as his *Disintegrating Connections* was the source for the distended rods projecting like antennae from the head of *Reclining Figure* (1935).

[27] The imagery of figures bound together with fish on a human scale is also reminiscent of Beckmann. See *Fourth Estate of the Free Press.*

51
The Rape. 1945.
Bronze, 9 × 5⅜ × 3½
inches. Collection Mr.
and Mrs. Stephen
Paine, Boston.
52
*Spectre Riding the
Golden Ass.* 1945.
Bronze, 11¾ × 12¼ ×
4 inches. Detroit
Institute of Art.

metal sculpture that Smith produced from 1945 to the end of the decade. All of Smith's
work during the middle and later 1940s was not, of course, volumetric. There was also
a sequence of sculpture devoted to the image of landscape expressed through linear
scaffolding counterpointed by pastoral motifs cut out of sheet metal. This second strain
ran concurrently with the compact bronzes. But it was the volumetric mode to which
Smith constantly returned to project the thematic strain of aggressiveness, brutality,
and death. Some obvious examples of the theme of violation from the year 1945 are
The Rape (Fig. 51), *War Landscape* (Fig. 39), *Spectre Riding the Golden Ass* (Fig. 52),
False Peace Spectre (Fig. 103), and *Perfidious Albion* (Fig. 114). The first two translate
the violation-by-cannon image of the *Medals* and drawings into bronze statuettes and
explore the theme with a carefully wrought naturalism. *The Rape* combines the winged
cannon/phallus with a nude sprawled along the ground, her upper torso raised by her
bent arms, her head pendant from her arched neck, her hair flowing to the ground behind
her. We immediately recognize the Giacometti *Woman with Her Throat Cut* that Smith
had repeatedly explored in his *Reclining Figures* of the 1930s. But the slender fins and
bent sheets of metal that had earlier constituted Smith's very personal translation of the
image have given way here to a solidly conventional rendering of the figures.

Similarly, the terms "conventional" and "solid" describe the formal qualities, if not the
imagery, of *Spectre Riding the Golden Ass.* Another small bronze of 1945, this work,
like *The Rape,* combines two smoothly modeled figures: a donkeylike animal kneeling
on its two front legs, bearing on its back a standing, hunched creature with a horn
in its mouth. The torso and "head" of this mounted figure resemble the cannon/phallus
from the *Medals* and support the outspread wings of the antique model Smith had
used before. The classical reference here is even stronger than it had been in previous
works, because the wrinkled breasts hanging from the chest of the spectre and the
eyeless character of the head suggest an identification of this creature as Tiresias, the
blind seer of classical mythology. But in fact it is not necessary to look outside Smith's
work for the source of this figure. Within the mythic cycle of Smith's own sculpture,
the constellation of a figure riding a tamed animal issues from the *Medals,* espe-

53·
*Medal for Dishonor:
Propaganda for
War.* 1939–1940.
Bronze, 11⅜ × 9⅜
inches. Joseph H.
Hirshhorn Collection,
New York.

Page from Sketch-
book #41. 1944–1954.
Archive IV/32.

cially *Propaganda for War* (Fig. 53). Smith's description of this medal had begun: "The
rape of the mind by machines of death. . . . Atop the curly bull the red cross nurse
blows the clarinet. The horse is dead in this bullfight arena—the bull is docile, can be
ridden."[28] According to this libretto for the medal, the idea of intellectual seduction
by means of propaganda is carried by the image of an Amazonlike woman seated on
an immobile animal, piping "emotional bombings" through a "corny trumpet." Thus,
in the very first medal of the series, Smith had directly focused on the theme that
underlines the whole group.

Insofar as the complete cycle of the *Medals* satirizes in deadly earnest the perversion
of an entire art form—the intaglio relief—that takes place when medals are cast to honor
"heroic" war deeds, the first medal serves as a preface to the set as a whole. But Smith
operates in the cycle with characteristic ambivalence, for his own images in the medals
participate imaginatively in the very acts of violence and mutilation he otherwise fervently wished to denounce. Further, the formal vocabulary of the *Medals* appears as
a regression from the modernist preoccupations of Smith's style in the 1930s to an
overtly comic-book or cartoonlike mode, with its exaggeration of the sexuality of the
women and its fidelity to the details of uniforms and weapons.[29] Thus a low or
burlesque style accompanies the satirical tone of the *Medals*, but both this comic-
book style and the occasional identification with the enemy appear as uninvited guests.
One witnesses a peculiar situation in the *Medals*, for they represent a debase-
ment of style and tone that runs counter to Smith's ostensible intentions.

Smith's own ambivalence makes all art somewhat suspect to him. He writes: "The

[28] Smith's notes for this *Medal* continue: "The stage is set—not for the first story of Jonah but for
the present Fish story—propaganda."
[29] See Drawing IV/32 (Fig. 54). As an adolescent, Smith had had his first taste of renown within
the small community in which he grew up when he earned the nickname Bud in high school.
Bud (for the cartoonist Bud Fisher) was given to Smith when, after taking a correspondence
course in cartooning, he demonstrated his own flair in this medium. The drawings for the *Medals*
appear in Smith's sketchbook side by side with cartoonlike renderings of circus figures and grotesques. See III/836, 1018, 858.

55
Untitled. 1955. Clay,
10 × 5¼ × 4½ inches.
Estate of the artist.

association of art with the graven and golden image . . . makes art taboo."[30] However much he was later to reject an art of sensuality and possession, he understood the absorption of his own art with the primitivism associated with the golden calf when he suggested that "beauty is to expose the cruelty in man"[31] and asked, "How long does it take crudities to become beauties?"[32] In both the *Medals* and the *Spectres* there is the feeling that for Smith exposure of "the cruelty in man" meant self-exposure.

 It is within this context that we can begin to corner the elusive meaning of the *Spectre Riding the Golden Ass*. When Smith sold it to the Detroit Institute, he refused to give its meaning to its new owner. In reply to the Institute's request for an explanation of the work, he stated only that he was interested in "the recurring myth," that he looked at all the cuneiform translations he could find, and that he read myths and their analyses.[33] But the *Spectre Riding* is probably not an illustration of a single myth taken from another culture. Rather, it blends primordial characters into an amalgam directed at Smith's own emotional life. In the *Spectre* the phallus is once more a sheathing or mask for the artist's personality. which "speaks" not merely through the horn projecting from its own mouth, but out of the ass's mouth as well, for the horn begins in the mouth of the spectre, passes down to the snout of the supporting animal and issues finally out of the open mouth of the donkey. In the *Propaganda* medal, the role of the golden ass had been played by a bull tamed to serve the purposes of false art. As I have said, Smith refers to a taboo art associated with the "golden image" or golden calf. The spectre becomes, by substitution, a false muse seducing Smith into an art that would serve false gods, an art that would become mired in preoccupations with violence and untransformed sexuality. However, the spectre in this work recalls the drawings of the phallic masks, so the notion of the false muse should be qualified to

[30] "Art and Religion," p. 11.
[31] See Archive III/982. This was written in 1945.
[32] From his 1954 College Art Association speech. See Archive IV/428. In 1952 Smith had written, "The beauties of nature do not conceal destruction and degeneration. Form will flower with spikes of steel, the savage idols of basic patterns." IV/361.
[33] See Letter I/363 in Detroit Archives.

56
36 Birdheads. 1950.
Steel, blue aluminum
paint, 55 × 36¼ inches.
Collection Mr. and Mrs.
Lee N. Baker, Baltimore.

57
Tanktotem I. 1952.
Steel, 90 × 39 inches.
Art Institute of
Chicago.

account for the reflexive nature of Smith's image. As an assertion of Smith's fantasies of aggression, the spectre becomes the artist literally speaking out of the mouth of his sculpture, the artist corporealized in subjects that were for at least a part of him considered taboo.

The endless spiral of Smith's conflicting emotions is relevant here to the extent that it points up the repetitive character of the content of Smith's imagery. The actual rape-by-cannon image was not confined to the production of 1945. He repeated it as late as 1955 in a series of small clay figures (see Fig. 55). Similarly, the cannon/phallus runs like a leitmotif through all the work of the 1940s and almost without alteration into the early 1950s.[34] (Another related theme that first appeared in the 1930s had to do with human sacrifice and was repeated with obsessive regularity in the 1940s, finally to be apotheosized into a broader formal conception in the 1950s.) But the sculpture of 1945, like the *Spectre Riding* and *The Rape,* shows that the particular forms Smith used to insist on these themes were volumetric in character. They were images couched in the language of stone carving and bronze casting, a language remote from Smith's identity as a welder.[35] Not only were the symbols conceived as a kind of visual mask,

[34] Examples are: *Spectre of War* (Fig. 101), 1944; *Jurassic Bird* (Fig. 102), *False Peace Spectre* (Fig. 103), and *Pillar of Sunday* (Fig. 68), all 1945; *Eagle's Lair* (Fig. 67), 1948; *Royal Incubator* (Fig. 66) and *36 Birdheads* (Fig. 56) (Smith also referred to this work as "36 Peckerheads"), both 1950; and *Tanktotems I* and *II* (Figs. 57 and 135), 1952. See Drawings, Archive IV/81–89 (Fig. 116). Smith wrote a poem related to *Tanktotem I* (Archive IV/742) that may be of interest in this connection:

to use the forms of cultivation
to erect and uphold the body of irrelevant cause
for the pleasure of pour
the graceful elevation of peckerheads
to extract and pour—the catharsis
the custom of pouring
sacrifice and blood-letting
the pouring off of living liquid
by the bird head
the external tract
the suggestion by body function of elimination
and its ritual lost from taboo

58
Daumier. *My Veloci-
pede!* Lithograph
published in *Charivari,*
September 17, 1868.
Tacked on a window
mullion in Smith's liv-
ing room at Bolton
Landing.
59
Woman in a Room.
1945. Bronze, 12 x 9¼
inches. Estate of the
artist.

but even the formal language issued as though by ventriloquy from a source different
from that of the constructed steel idiom of his work in the 1930s. They were therefore
far from the tone in which Smith had originally stated his artistic identity: the voice of
a welder, which was ultimately—and he himself was aware of the double meaning—
the voice of a smith.

The Landscapes of
the Fifties

In 1951 David Smith made *Hudson River Landscape* (Fig. 60) and *The Banquet* (Fig. 29).
Shallow, rectilinear, weblike, their flat facades knifing across the viewer's line of sight,
these sculptures were radically unlike the human body with its density and its upright
verticality. In that sense they seemed to his critics to represent Smith's breakthrough;
it was as though his originality, his claim to modernism, could be identified with the
rejection of the human figure. Cleaving to the idea of landscape, Smith was seen as
entering into modernism by means of a format that was horizontal rather than vertical
and referred to continuous space rather than mass or volume. Yet the great sculptures of
the 1950s, the *Agricolas,* the *Tanktotems,* and the *Sentinels,* are all upright, and they
insinuate the form of the human body, although certainly not its density or volume.
Nothing that has anything to do with landscape sculpture has much relevance to these
works. The relation of linear segments to a frame, the lateral deployment of planes
with reference to a horizon line, the tremendous variability of the image itself, all
may be characteristic of sculpture striving for an allusion to landscape, but the great
Smiths of the fifties cannot be characterized in this way. Sullenly unexpansive, rigidly

the logic to pour water off boiled potatoes
the liquid to solids for essences
At the end of his life Smith owned two full-sized working cannons. One was a Revolutionary
War model, the other a cannon cast in bronze. See *David Smith* (Marlborough-Gerson Gallery,
New York, October 1964), p. 7.
[35] Some of Smith's monolithic sculptures were highly dependent on the specific work of other
artists as well as on an imported formal language. One case of this is the 1945 *Woman in a Room,*
which is closely derived from Picasso's *Girl before a Mirror* (1932), as well as from his 1932 Boisgeloup
sculptures of female heads. This last group also appears to be the source of the handling of parts
of *Sedate Figure* and *Adagio Dancers* (both 1945). See Fig. 59.

60
Hudson River Landscape. 1951. Steel and stainless steel, 49½ × 75 × 16¼ inches. Whitney Museum of American Art, New York.

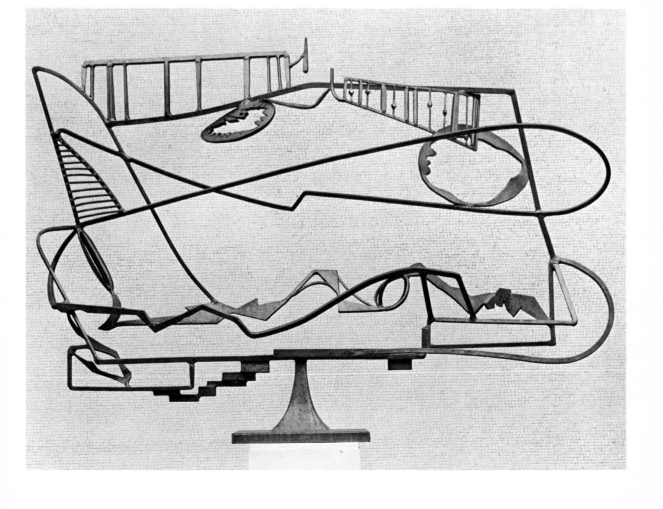

61
Tanktotem VII. 1960.
Steel, painted blue,
dark blue, and white,
84½ × 36¾ × 14⅛
inches. Storm King
Art Center, Moun-
tainville, New York.
62
Voltri-Bolton V.
1962. Steel, drybrushed
with orange paint,
86½ × 34 × 24 inches.
Collection Mr. and
Mrs. John Braston,
San Francisco.

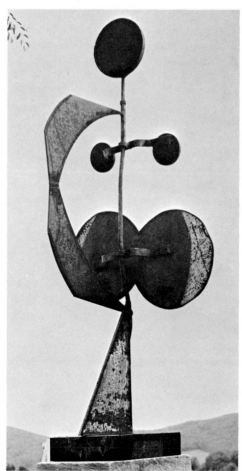

erect, these works almost compulsively repeat the same basic configuration: a planar, frontal torso; a schematic head; a tripodlike connection with the ground. It is a configuration that, from its first entrance into his work in 1945, Smith called "totem."

It might be asked why, in the masterpieces of his mature work, Smith succumbed to what was at bottom so figurative an idea, when, from the earliest years of his career, he appears to have been drawn to and convinced by a formal language that was highly abstract. Yet a close look at Smith's full production will reveal that he resolved each of his sculptures in terms of one of about four images that he repeated through almost the whole of his artistic life. These themes became for Smith the point of intersection between his personal concerns and feelings and his convictions about form. For this reason, before turning to those magnificent, upright objects of the 1950s, all of them pulling toward the gravitational field of the totem image, it seems to me important to look briefly at Smith's activity during the later 1940s. At that time Smith was forcing the solid mode of the early forties into an ever more subsidiary role within his work and struggling to reopen the path he had followed during the innovative campaign of the 1930s. To this end he challenged the heavy, smoothly modeled, closed forms of works like *Spectre Riding* and *The Rape* with a far more linear and open style, which he used for the depiction of landscape.

Knowing that Smith was headed toward a sculpture of increasing abstractness and immateriality in the 1950s, there is a temptation to picture Smith's work during the forties as simply divided into two ranges of production, the first and more important (in terms of his future development) committing him to a radical exploration of open sculpture, the second, and, from this point of view, less important, being the sequence of small-scale, retrograde work that repeated the themes touched on before, themes that left unresolved the brutality Smith directed at outside objects, whether at the sculpture itself or at the viewer. It is clear from the vantage point of the present that the landscape series begun in 1946 and culminating in the open-skein pieces of 1951 was a kind of rope ladder by which Smith pulled himself up and out of a pit of confused subjectivity. However, to define the landscapes as Smith's salvation and his breakthrough is already to have a very particular idea of what he broke through to.[36] As I have tried to indicate, this idea does not really leave room for the facts about Smith's performance in the greatest of his sculpture. If, however, one sees the landscapes as only a provisional solution—as a way out but certainly not *the* way—one sees Smith's later career in profoundly different terms. I have been maintaining that Smith's turn toward landscape was a turning away from the pursuit of the object, the solid, unitary form as the focus for either aggression or desire. This strategy, which is like the self-administration of an antidote to the powerful drug of fantasy, reminds one of Cézanne's undertaking in the early 1870s, when he too submerged himself in landscape through an apprenticeship to Impressionism. But as I have indicated before, landscape was to prove an eventual dead end for Smith in that it seemed to avoid rather than solve the problem of the object. It is impossible to offer any specific proof for this assertion beyond the fact that Smith returned, via the totem, to an utterly transformed presentation of the sculptural object, a presentation that no longer circumvented the question of possession but could now test issues central to sculpture itself. However, it *is* possible to show in what way landscape brought Smith to an impasse in his formal development, and this is important to an understanding of the kind of formal decisions he made after his brief and rather brilliant manipulation of the two-dimensional format of the landscape image.

Beginning with *Helmholtzian Landscape*[37] in 1946 and continuing through the pastoral

[36] For a discussion of the question of "breakthrough" in modernist painting, see Michael Fried, "The Achievement of Morris Louis," *Artforum* 5 (February 1967): 34-40.

[37] In a speech he wrote in 1947 and delivered at Skidmore College (on February 17), Smith invoked the idea of the parallel between Impressionist painting and the studies of light made by Chevreul and Helmholtz (IV/320). In addition to this reference to Helmholtz in 1947, there is a later one from a speech at the Corcoran Gallery of Art in Washington. "The coloring of carved form was a supplementary factor in the identification of the object," Smith said in 1951. "The gradual substitution of indicated form for actual form imprisoned the painting concept until its scientific release by Helmholtz, its pictorial release by the invention of the camera, its conceptual release by impressionism." Archive I/1058.

63
Helmholtzian Landscape. 1946. Painted steel, 15⅞ × 17⅜ × 7⅛ inches. Collection David Lloyd Kreeger, Washington, D.C.

works of 1951 like *Hudson River Landscape*, Smith demanded that his sculpture exchange the isolated object for an image of deep space. All of these works seek immateriality and openness, and the way they attempt this is by means of a direct reference to painting. For if the medium of sculpture makes the object accessible to the viewer as an object, this is not the case in painting, since painting by its very nature sets the object beyond the viewer's grasp.

In *Helmholtzian Landscape* (Fig. 63) flat sheets of foliage extend laterally along the same plane occupied by a profile figure and an enclosing frame. Together these elements establish a continuous surface that we associate immediately with the plane of a picture. In front of and behind the foliage sheets, Smith projects small animal and floral shapes that either cover or are themselves covered by the opaque sheets of the supporting forms. Therefore the viewer, forced by the rigid frontality of the sculpture to stand directly before it, cannot see the whole assembly of landscape elements. Instead he is aware that there are relationships among parts of the sculpture buried within the "illusionistic" space behind the "picture plane" that are visually inaccessible to him. The imagery of the sculpture itself reenacts this dilemma by showing the man in the landscape in profile, standing before the display of organic forms that would overlap one another from his viewing point and would therefore be invisible to him, since they lie hidden "inside" the sculpture's depicted forest. The work itself displays a cross section of the observer's visual field. In this way it recreates or illustrates the intellectualist doubts about sculpture, the turn-of-the-century fears about the cheat of normal vision. In front of *Helmholtzian Landscape* we feel that we are back again in the ambience of the Futurist sculpture of Boccioni or Gabo's Constructivism. Visual apprehension of the object is offered diagrammatically (a cross section spread over the picture plane), while the actual objects of sight are masked by each other. Thus the pictorial context of this work opens up the sculpture only to close it off again behind the surface of the traditional picture. The model Smith used in *Helmholtzian Landscape* is the transparent, illusionistic picture surface. Insofar as this is the premodernist concept of the picture surface—the strategy we see operating in Hildebrand and Rosso

—Smith's action in the landscapes is symbolically rather than actually radical.

This in itself should prompt us to reassess the characterization of the schism in Smith's work during the forties. Instead of pointing to those two parallel modes as a split between a more and a less advanced sculptural language, we should probably view the two strains as simply a more and a less sublimated gesture toward possession. The landscapes of the 1940s seem merely to represent the other side of the physically violent, sensuous possession acted out in the contemporaneous solid works. By making comprehension depend on a diagrammatic rendering of the object, they return to the aloof omniscience of the Hildebrand perspective. As long as the surfaces of these works ask to be read as traditional picture surfaces, they heighten rather than reduce the mystery of the objects contained within them. The development of the objects takes place illusionistically behind the surface and deprives the work of that total openness to view, laden with its attendant contingencies, that Smith had earlier and would subsequently assert as the stuff of sight itself.

The landscapes that followed *Helmholtzian Landscape* continued to evoke the traditional pictorial field, both by aligning their steel calligraphy along a continuous two-dimensional plane and by using a frame to enclose the work. By framing these sculptures, Smith literally locates them within a pictorial context, just as Picasso had in the constructions of 1914 that were a fundamental part of Smith's radical artistic heritage. Like Picasso, Smith imports into this assembly conventions that refer to depth: in *The Letter* (Fig. 64), Smith's signature, cut out of sheet steel, begins at a point on the circular base of the work that is well in advance of the major plane of the sculpture and arcs backward into that plane, referring to the relation between signature and illusion in painting. Calling attention to itself as something written on an actual surface rather than something that resides in space behind that surface, a painter's signature often momentarily disrupts the persuasiveness of the pictorial illusion. In *The Letter* the signature is exploited as a sign pointing to the pictorial nature of the rest of the work by means of its own nakedly material existence in the viewer's space in front of the sculpture. It thrusts the images of the work into an illusionist space. The analogy be-

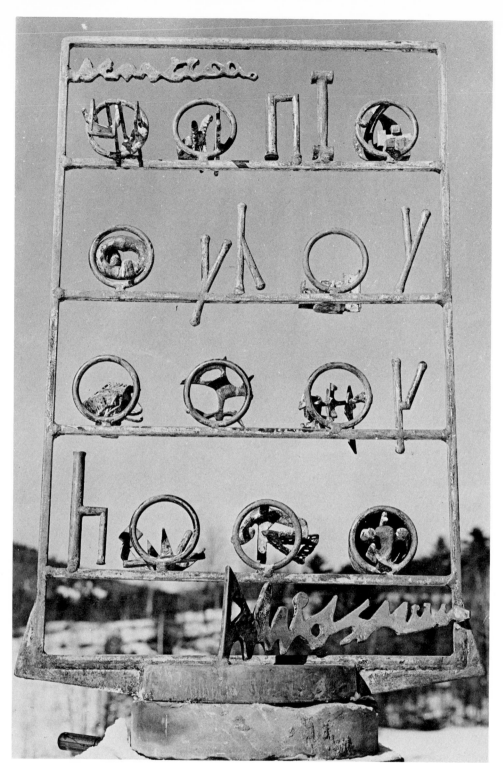

64
The Letter. 1950.
Welded steel, 37⅝ ×
22⅞ × 9¼ inches.
Munson-Williams-
Proctor Institute,
Utica, New York.

tween Smith's landscape and Picasso's sculpture of 1914 stops at this point. In annexing the surface of painting to his constructions, Picasso ensures that the shape of the bottles or guitars or other still-life elements of the work will seem to be dependent on its surface, so that the shape itself becomes the result of the artist's prerogative to affirm the surface of the work of art. The defining silhouette of the object does not have the quality of a thing known in advance of the experience of the sculpture but is discovered in the vision of it.

Initially, Smith's objective in *The Letter* may have been similar to Picasso's. Indeed, the theme of the work suggests it, for *The Letter* was to consist of a message discovered in seeing it, not of a familiar set of objects whose shapes the sculptor merely represents. But this relationship between shape and surface is not achieved in *The Letter* for two reasons. First, because the contour of the sculpture, being a rectangle, a picture frame, is known in advance; like Boccioni's bottle or Gabo's ideal volumes, the enclosing contour is set by the exigencies of representation rather than the logic of the formal relationships manifested at the work's surface. Second, the imagery inside the frame remains depicted and furtive. It is not made legible within the context of the sculpture but reads like a set of secret glyphs for which the viewer has no key. We may recognize the fetus from *Growing Forms* (Fig. 65) and *The Royal Incubator* (Fig. 66), the actual bird image from the landscapes of 1945 and 1946, and the bird/cannon image from works of the 1940s like *The Rape, Eagle's Lair* (Fig. 67), and *Pillar of Sunday* (Fig. 68), but *The Letter* maintains these images as representations of the past, hermetically closed off behind the imagined picture surface. By staying within the limits of an illusionistic picture, openness to vision becomes entirely fictional. The surface, as in the landscapes of the 1940s, is made into a film behind which the "real" objects lie. This is even spelled out in *The Letter* by the fact that the actual images crouch behind individual frames. They must be peered at through circular openings that contain the images much the way a linear contour on the surface of a painting contains the illusory existence that lies behind it.[38]

38 For a discussion of the imagery of *The Letter,* see Chapter 3, fn. 16.

65
Growing Forms
1939. Cast aluminum,
28 × 9 × 6 inches.
Estate of the artist.

66
Royal Incubator. 1950.
Steel, bronze, and
silver, 37 × 38⅜ ×
9⅞ inches. Estate of
the artist.

67
Eagle's Lair. 1948.
Steel and bronze, 33¾
× 17¼ × 13 inches.
Estate of the artist.

68
Pillar of Sunday. 1945.
Steel, painted pink,
30½ × 18 × 9½ inches.
Estate of the artist.

The Totem

Shortly after finishing *Hudson River Landscape,* Smith was to repudiate the specific imitation of the picture, first in *Australia* and then in the *Agricolas* and *Tanktotems.* *Australia* (Fig. 69) is the first of the monumental pieces of the 1950s that does not depend on the suggestion of a picture frame to set its contour. Instead, Smith situates separate pockets of figuration around the edge of the sculptural body. Inside is an open field that reads as a transparent membrane or continuous surface, while aggregations of straps that undulate through space or extend out into it establish the perimeter. In speaking of the inside of the body as opposed to its outside, I am not merely raising, in masked form, the intellectualist inside-outside question. The inside of the work is not the hidden interior of a three-dimensional whole, miraculously revealed by a kind of x-ray vision, and the outside of the work, its shape, does not rely on the a priori geometric edge of Constructivism or the enclosing rectangle of the picture frame. In *Australia* Smith pulls back from a simple contour, but at the same time he concentrates all of the visual activity of the work at its edge. *Australia* happens at the boundary between what is the sculpture and what is not.

Unlike the works that precede it, *Australia* situates its pictorial incident not *within* its perimeter but *at* its perimeter. By shifting the sections of density away from the center of the sculpture and massing incident at the edges, Smith makes the viewer uncertain about the shape of the work. Smith's decision in *Australia* was to exchange the enclosing shape possessed by objects in the world for an exclusively sculptural shape, which meant making it seem to be generated by the accessibility of the surface.

The meaning of Smith's determination during the 1950s to focus attention on a radical view of surface is that through it total accessibility to vision could become the subject of his sculpture, much the way that illusionism had become the "subject" in Analytic Cubism.[39] Just as in Cubism one no longer confronts the illusion of something, so in the sculpture David Smith now wanted to make, the observer no longer experiences the surface as the surface of something. Instead, the surface makes the work visually accessible, while defeating the desire for possession by touch. It is this knowability

[39] See Clement Greenberg, *Art and Culture* (Boston: Beacon Press, 1962), p. 79.

69
Australia. 1951. Steel,
painted brown, 79¾
× 107 × 16¾ inches.
Collection William S.
Rubin, New York.

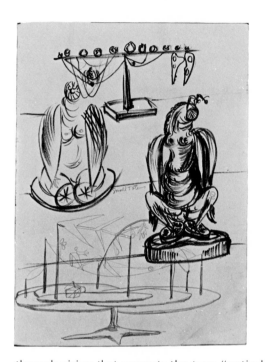

70
Page from Sketchbook
#41. 1944–1954. Ar-
chive IV/81.

through vision that suggests the term "optical," rather than any literal transparency or denial of surface. Clement Greenberg characterized modernist sculpture as giving rise to "the illusion not of things, but of modalities, namely that matter is incorporeal, weightless, and exists only optically, like a mirage."[40] At first this seems an apology for total linearism in sculpture, because line would appear to be the proper agent of weight-lessness and incorporeality. Since a steel line, especially one curved back on itself, straddles in our experience the modalities of two- and three-dimensionality, "sculpture can confine itself to virtually two dimensions (as some of David Smith's pieces do) without being felt to violate the limitations of its medium, because the eye recognizes that what offers itself in two dimensions is actually (not palpably) fashioned in three."[41] But line did not become Smith's medium; rather, he took as his medium a new concept of surface capable of enforcing conditions of seeing that would expose the real nature of our attempts to grasp objects and the quality of their grip on us, making tangible the cost of traversing the distance between the viewer and the object he would possess.

Although the title *Australia* might suggest yet another landscape image, the far-flung shape of the work depicts a kangaroo, the aboriginal totem animal of Australia. It is not clear whether Smith's interest in the symbolism of non-Western cultures preceded or followed his acquaintance with the psychoanalytic interpretations of totemic prac-tice.[42] But whatever the actual sequence in the development of Smith's thought, it is certain that by the later 1940s he was fully aware of the connection Freud's *Totem and Taboo* makes between primitive ritual and constraints on behavior in modern societies.[43]

[40] Ibid., p. 144.
[41] Ibid., p. 143.
[42] In a sketchbook of the 1940s, Smith began to draw "small totems." See Archive IV/81–85 (Fig. 70).
[43] Conversation with Dorothy Dehner, who has also spoken of Smith's general knowledge of psycho-analytic theory at this time. In 1946 Dorothy Dehner introduced Smith to Dr. Bernard Glueck, a former analysand of Freud who summered near Glens Falls. The analyst and Smith became good friends; according to Miss Dehner's report, Dr. Glueck spent hours with Smith in his studio while Smith worked and they talked together. Although Miss Dehner says that he had already read the book in the late forties, Smith wrote to Tom Hess in 1953, asking him to send a copy of Kris's *Psychoanalytic Explorations into Art* (Archive V/717), and shortly after this Smith went to see Kris

In Smith's hands the idea of the totem became the thematic bridge between the emotions that grip the volumetric works of the 1940s and the still inarticulate formal content of the landscapes. For the theme of the totem combines the desire for contact (as the overture to violation) and the prohibition against possession. In totem-worshiping societies the totem is the most tabooed object because, in Freud's view, it stood for the things most desired by the male members of the clan. A clansman's relation to the totem is ambivalent, for the totem is not just the external object of a clan's elaborate set of prohibitions against touching, killing, or eating; the totem is internalized in that its name refers to the clansmen as well. For the Australian tribesman the kangaroo is both an external object—the taboo animal—and his identity as a member of the clan. He is a Kangaroo; and this identification, which makes outbreeding obligatory, fixes the distance between him and the females of the same name.

The sexual taboo expressed in the totem object was important for Smith's special use of the theme, for from it Smith expanded modern sculpture's earlier passive admiration for primitive or archetypal forms into an active and emotional relationship between the viewer and the work of art. Smith's demand that the spectator acknowledge and come to grips with the fixed viewing point stems from reasons that go beyond his evident distaste for the conceptual timidity of that sculpture generally acknowledged to be modern. In forcing the spectator to recognize his own fixity before the sculpture, Smith hoped to gain leverage on the issues that surround the desire to possess the object, either intellectually or through ownership.

It is relatively easy to document the dual identity of Smith's totem sculpture as both an object located at a fixed distance from the sculptor/viewer and as a manifestation of his own person. One instance concerns a work of 1951–1952 called *The Hero* (Fig. 71). Standing over six feet high, the spare, simple elements compose a rigidly frontal, female totem. Rising from a notched pedestal, a thin, irregular shaft supports a lozenge-shaped disc that defines the head, and a rectangular frame that establishes the torso,

---

professionally. Smith's second wife, Jean Freas Smith, told me that they had only one consultation, during which Smith was advised against an analysis.

71
The Hero. 1951–1952.
Steel, painted red, 73⅝
× 25½ × 11¾ inches.
Brooklyn Museum.

72
Sitting Printer. 1954.
Bronze, 87½ × 15½ ×
15 inches. Storm King
Art Center, Mountain-
ville, New York.

within which two protrusions from the central shaft read as incipient breasts and provide the only descriptive release from the terse geometry of the figure. (Not only is
the *Hero* a female figure, but the *Tanktotems*—the series whose title most openly pro-
claims Smith's preoccupation with the notion of totemism—also assert their identity as
females. In those sculptures Smith constantly uses the circular, convex form of the
boiler heads that give the series its name to locate the pelvic region of the figures.
Smith was later to comment that he never made "boy sculptures.")[44] In a poem about
The Hero, Smith said:

the subject is me
the hero is eye function
the image doesn't lead
the morality is above
the work, or below
but never with.[45]

However, the ambiguous attachment of a male name to a female sculpture is consistent with the Freudian explanation of totemism, in which the male's identity—his
clan name—is synonymous with the prohibited female object. As I have already noted,
Smith's understanding of totemic practice was drawn largely from psychoanalytic sources.
 Just as in the 1930s and 1940s Smith repeated the violated female and the violating
cannon/phallus with an almost obsessive insistency, so in the 1950s and 1960s he continually reiterated this image of the hero/totem. Significantly, the sculptured restatements
always took the same form: a linearly supported rectangular and planar torso surmounted
by a geometric head, the whole expressed with an insistent bilateral symmetry. Two
examples from the period 1950-1960 are *Sitting Printer* (Fig. 72) and *Tanktotem IX* (Fig.

[44] This was said in a television interview between Smith and Frank O'Hara:
O'Hara: "You must feel that there are all these strange objects around you, in your whole studio
or outside."
Smith: "Well, they're all girl sculptures. Oh, they're all girls. . . . I don't make boy sculptures."
(See Bibliography, no. 60.)
[45] Archive IV/989.

73
Cubi II. 1963. Stain-
less steel, 130½ ×
36⅞ × 23⅞ inches.
Estate of the artist.
74
Cubi VI. 1963. Stain-
less steel, 118⅛ × 29½
× 21¾ inches. Estate
of the artist.

75). (Sculptures from the *Voltri–Bolton Landing* series [Figs. 126 and 128] and a few of the *Cubis* [Figs. 73, 74, 93, and 146] carry this image into the 1960s.)[46] Although this anthropomorphic framework was itself unchanging, Smith was continually putting pressure on his formal ideas to expand and develop. To experience the change from the early totems to the later ones, we might consider the development up through *Tanktotem IX* (1960), a late work that repeats *The Hero* almost part for part.

Graphically *The Hero* relates to *Hudson River Landscape, Australia,* and others among its contemporaries. The handling of steel as line is similar to other works of 1951. In *The Hero* we see clearly the price Smith had to pay for initially basing his claim to openness on the effectiveness of line. In order to appear as line rather than as scaffolding, Smith's steel bands, as in the central stem of *The Hero,* must remain figurative, descriptive, allusive. It is to this end that he bends and pinches the metal rod or extrudes it to indicate the breasts that project into the spare form of the torso. Looking at the open rectangular shape itself, we read the widening of the steel ribbon at the top right as shoulder. As these allusions to the human body mount up, each perception seems to add a specific weight and density to that part of the sculpture until the work begins to appear swaddled in the conceptual bulk of depicted flesh. Thus, reduction of the sculpture to line does not win abstraction for Smith, since line remains as intractably figurative as it had in painting before the Pollocks of 1947–1950.[47]

[46] Smith began to deal with this theme as early as 1945. The repetitive structure of *Pillar of Sunday,* a work from that year, clearly suggests the totem-pole image, and such an identification is made explicit by Smith himself in a drawing for the sculpture published in the catalogue to the Willard/Buchholz exhibition in 1946. This sculpture and *Perfidious Albion* were the first totems to appear in Smith's art. (See Chapter 3, fn. 14.) The totems that abounded in Smith's production were always female. *Pillar of Sunday* seems to refer to his mother, as had *Widow's Lament* and *Reliquary House* (Fig. 68). One of the things that symptomized his family's conventionality for Smith was his mother's participation in the local Methodist church, which, among other activities, involved her in teaching Sunday school. Miss Dehner said that Smith often referred to his mother derisively as "the pillar of the church."

[47] See Michael Fried's important discussion of this topic in *Three American Painters* (Cambridge, Mass.: Fogg Museum, 1965), pp. 10–15.

75
Tanktotem IX. 1960.
Steel, painted blue,
white, and red, 90¾
× 30¾ × 24⅛ inches.
Estate of the artist.

Smith's figurative line of the early 1950s not only demands an allusive reading but also calls for a pedestal, something to serve as a transition between the ground on which we stand and the wholly different realm of the sculpture. Clement Greenberg speaks of line in modernist sculpture as having to support nothing but itself, but in *The Hero* (as in *Hudson River Landscape* and *The Banquet*), Smith's line is called on to "support" figuration.

Shortly after 1951 Smith repudiated this quality of line as specific drawing. By 1960, in *Tanktotem IX* (Fig. 75), we can see the formal distance Smith had traveled during the decade of the 1950s. This piece is composed, like *The Hero*, of a linear stem (an attenuated tripod), a rectangular torso (a solid steel plate painted white), and a semicircular head (half the top of a boiler tank). In *Tanktotem IX* Smith's line is no longer the cursive stroke that "supports nothing but itself"; instead, line functions to hold up the plane of the body. Yet paradoxically it is in the very role of physical support that the logic of support is put under formal scrutiny, since at the juncture between plate and tripod there is no expression of weight. The line slips by manifestly at the front of the work (and, by implication, at the back of it), and the line is read against the plane as a pictorial element. For the first time, Smith's line becomes fully abstract, as the distinction between a physical mode (structure in itself) and a formal one (the properties of line) becomes the source of tension in the work.

At the same time, the flat plane of *Tanktotem IX* establishes itself as torso-become-surface. The surface seems legible as the whole object, since everything there is to know about the work is given to the eye in this reading. Everything has literally been made into surface, leaving no possibilities for the distinction between interior and exterior that had clung to Smith's earlier work, either because a quality of inside and outside had adhered to his still representational line or because of a sense of interior, no matter how vestigial, had remained to the sculpture as a whole because of its allusiveness. In achieving the surfaceness of *Tanktotem IX*, Smith achieves the surfaceness of painting, the conviction that everything in the work is coextensive with the surface, at last accessible to sight.

The meaning of *Tanktotem IX* has to do, it seems to me, with the felt difference between visual and physical accessibility. The very act of concentrating on the surface—and with *Tanktotem IX* this is the same as saying the act of looking at the sculpture—induces a rather specialized way of seeing objects. By forcing the viewer to read the body in *Tanktotem IX* totally as surface, Smith promotes the situation that analytic psychology generalized as possible for all perception (but that Merleau-Ponty shows to be irrelevant to normal perception).[48] This is the attitude called "attention," by means of which the perceiver can theoretically correct the kinds of misinformation that give rise to optical illusions. By forcing himself to abstract details of his visual field from their context and view them in isolation, a subject can, for example, really see that the two lines in the Müller-Lyer illusion[49] are actually equal in length, just as by looking at it through a cardboard tube, he can see that the moon is the same size at the horizon as at its zenith. Conversely, the subject can be made to see that the two pieces of white paper, one in light and the other in shadow, that he normally identifies as the same are in fact differently colored: one white, the other gray. Yet these very acts of perception are a kind of abstraction. They force the observer to abandon his perception of the whole object and to concentrate arbitrarily on its secondary qualities or properties: color or texture. In the act of seeing in this specialized way the object loses its density and becomes miragelike. Its surface becomes the totality of the experience, because it is a surface detached from any object that could resonate meaning through it. This kind of looking does not occur in normal perception but can be induced, as it regularly is in perceptual tests. It is also induced by David Smith's sculpture, where the viewer's attention to surface and the shapes generated by it gives him the sensation of mirage that Greenberg was the first to apply to modern sculpture. The total coincidence of surface with the thing seen that we find in *Tanktotem IX* might suggest an explanation for Smith's nonchalant attitude toward the formal ques-

[48] Maurice Merleau-Ponty, *The Phenomenology of Perception* (London: Routledge and Kegan Paul, 1965), pp. 225 ff.
[49] The Müller-Lyer illusion was first published in 1889.

76
Table Torso. 1942.
Bronze, 10 × 4½ × 5⅝
inches. Rose Art Mu-
seum, Brandeis Uni-
versity, Waltham,
Massachusetts.
77
*Head as a Still Life
II.* 1942. Cast alumi-
num, 14 × 8½ × 4
inches. Estate of the
artist.

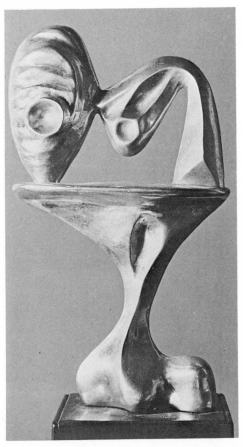

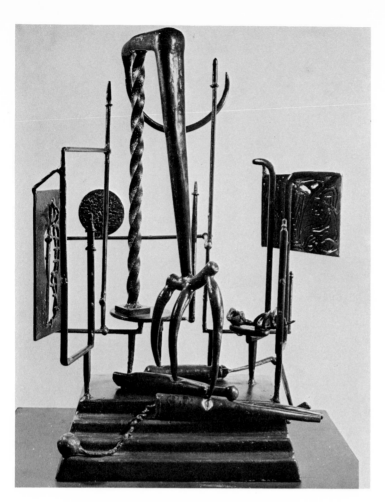

78
Cathedral. 1950. Steel, painted brown, 34⅛ × 24½ × 17⅛ inches. Estate of the artist.

tion of the propriety of painting steel sculpture. Once the entire experience of the three-dimensional object is directed away from its weight and density onto its secondary qualities, color, as an applied surface, is wholly unproblematic.

What is achieved in *Tanktotem IX*, then, is a complete fusion of formal and emotive content. In this work it is no accident that Smith locates the formal analysis of line at the pelvic region of the body, so that the tension between description and abstraction takes place in the region of the genitals. For Smith the demands of form were never formalistic. He wanted to identify sculpture as a physical object that can be possessed like any other object. But at the same time he wanted to qualify this definition of sculpture by putting a moral charge on the work of art, by differentiating it from the rest of the group of inert things that it would seem to belong to. The work of art is the repository for content in a way that mere physical objects are not. Smith analogizes this categorical distinction between it and the other members of its class to the moral distance that keeps men from making their fellows objects for possession.

In the seven years between its first heroic statement and the creation of *Tanktotem IX*, Smith had continually reworked the totem image, and each successive reincarnation seemed like a rephrasing of the problem, directed at new formal answers. If *Tanktotem IX* now seems an utterly lucid and compelling work of art, it apparently did not satisfy Smith. For *Tanktotem IX* was not the final resolution of this theme. The word "obsessive" was used earlier in connection with the persistence of the cannon/phallus image during the 1940s and its reappearance in the *Zigs* of the early 1960s. It was not used casually. Smith's return to certain formats—all of them aimed at the theme of desire for violent possession countered by a formal guarantee of protection to the object—suggests a correspondence with obsessional acts. What is meant here is not just the compulsion to repeat that characterizes obsessive behavior but the structure of the obsessive act itself. Freud characterized it as a ritual that first wards off the repressed wish but then becomes the act through which the repressed impulse may be expressed.[50] This

[50] Sigmund Freud, "Obsessive Acts and Religious Practices," in *Character and Culture* (New York: Crowell & Collier Macmillan, Collier Books, 1963), pp. 24 ff.

79
Sacrifice. 1950. Steel, painted red, 31⅝ × 19⅝ × 20⅞ inches. Estate of the artist.

formula for the growth of the compulsive act toward an ever more exacting metaphor for the suppressed desire suggests a parallel with Smith's own progression from the sadistic imagery of the 1940s to the totemic theme of the 1950s.

The totem and cannon/phallus were not the only images that Smith returned to obsessively. Human sacrifice and ritual burial were the two other major themes running through his career. Like the cannon/phallus they entered his work at an early stage, never to leave it. The first of these elaborated the idea of sacrifice by showing the victim anatomically wedded to the altar or table of ritual destruction.[51] *Table Torso* in 1942 (Fig. 76) was the earliest example, closely followed by a sequence of *Head as a Still Life* sculptures (Fig. 77). The idea was carried into the 1950s in works like *Cathedral* (Fig. 78),[52] *Sacrifice* (Fig. 79), and *The Banquet* (Fig. 29),[53] and into the later work in one of the *Sentinels* (Fig. 80), the *Voltri-Bolton Landing* tables, and some of the *Menand* (Fig. 84) and *Cubi* images.

The relation between the second theme, ritual burial, and its eventual formal statement is slightly more diffuse. Originally conceived as an image of protection and enclosure, it first appears in 1938 in *Growing Forms* (Fig. 65), where a fetus hangs in suspension within an enclosing but transparent capsule. (*Growing Forms* is not only the most derivative object Smith ever made[54] but also the preserve of concepts Smith

[51] The table torso is a recurrent theme in Smith's work. The body atop a table or platform is related to the sacrificial image of a body on an altar. Smith himself draws this parallel in his comments to Elaine de Kooning for her article, "David Smith Makes a Sculpture." The altar/sacrifice image first appears in the *Medals for Dishonor* (see Fig. 115) and is carried on into the 1940s and 1950s. Greatly abstracted and stripped of its specificity, it is behind the platform compositions of major works in the sixties, from the *Albany* and *Menand* series (e.g., Figs. 84 and 86), the *Voltri-Bolton Landing* sculptures (e.g., Figs. 81 and 85) and the *Cubis* (e.g., Fig. 143). During the 1940s, works like Figs. 77 and 79 had explicitly investigated the idea of parts of the body presented as a still life.
[52] See Smith's discussion of the "altar table," ibid.
[53] See drawings for *Sacrifice* and *The Banquet,* Archive III/1269, 1270, and 1122.
[54] The type for this sculpture was the commonest of the avant-garde sculptural currency in the late 1930s. Hepworth's and Moore's sculpture provide general examples. But there is probably a much more specific source for *Growing Forms,* although evidence for it must remain circumstantial. In 1938, Smith exhibited for the first time with the American Abstract Artists. In the same exhibition

had rejected in other contemporary sculpture. Locating the fetus within the interior of a womblike casing which is parted to reveal its normally concealed contents, *Growing Forms* operates at the level of the pseudo-Cubist problem raised by Boccioni's *Development of a Bottle,* discussed earlier.) The succession of sculpture that followed *Growing Forms* climaxed in *The Royal Incubator* of 1950 (Fig. 66). At the same time Smith was fascinated by the idea of the reliquary box, a container of the human figure in death.[55] Also carried within a protective casing, the relic is usually a fragment of a body. The canopic jar, which is an Egyptian parallel to the reliquary box, became the subject of a sculpture in 1951[56] and was the first version of the format through which this kind of subject matter joined the mainstream of Smith's development. The *Canopic Head* image (Fig. 90)—the stereometric projection of a volume combined with or defeated by bladelike planes or surfaces—was developed in *Agricola VIII* (Fig. 132), *Albany V* (Fig. 91), *Black White Backward, Circles and Arcs* (Fig. 92), *Compass Circle, Voltri XII,* and *Voltri-Bolton V* and *X* (Figs. 62 and 136), to name only a few.

The discussion of content in works of art, especially modern works of art, is some-times criticized as a vulgarization of the tools of analysis. This is certainly legitimate in cases where the naked act of pointing to the imagery of such objects is supposed to "explain" them, as, for example, when the historian or critic feels that by showing the various levels on which Picasso's *Guernica* enacts the themes of destruction and regen-eration he is also showing that the painting is a formally coherent object. In fact, while knowledge of *Guernica's* content may possibly make Picasso's motives accessible or even help to measure the scale of his ambitions for this painting, it is not in itself a gauge of the work's success as a formal statement.

Failure to make a discussion of content intersect the formal meanings of the sculp-tures themselves is the risk I run in examining David Smith's imagery, for merely to

---

was a work by Ibram Lassaw (Fig. 87)—plaster over wire armatures—that seems to forecast the shapes Smith would use in his work one year later.
[55] See sketchbook pages in Archive III/828 and 1039 (Fig. 107).
[56] Figure 89. See also Archive III/723, a 1942 sketch of a canopic jar.

80
Sentinel. 1961. Stainless steel, 106 × 23 × 16½ inches. Estate of the artist.

81
Voltri-Bolton XXIII.
1963. Steel, 69¼ × 24
× 25½ inches. Collection Miss Sara Dora
Greenberg, New York.
82
Voltri-Bolton XXIII.
(alternate view)

83
Albany XII. 1961.
Steel, painted black,
30 × 14½ × 21¼ in-
ches. Collection Mr.
and Mrs. Stephen
Paine, Boston.
84
Menand VI. 1963.
Steel, treated with acid,
34¼ × 20¼ × 17¼
inches. Collection Mr.
Wells Henderson,
Gladwyne, Pennsyl-
vania.
85
Voltri XVIII. 1962.
Steel, 42⅜ × 40 ×
32¾ inches. Estate of
the artist.
86
Albany III. 1959.
Steel, painted black,
26½ × 20 × 11¾
inches. Estate of the
artist.

87
Ibram Lassaw. *Sculpture.* 1936. Plaster on pipe and wire armature, 36 inches. Collection of the artist.

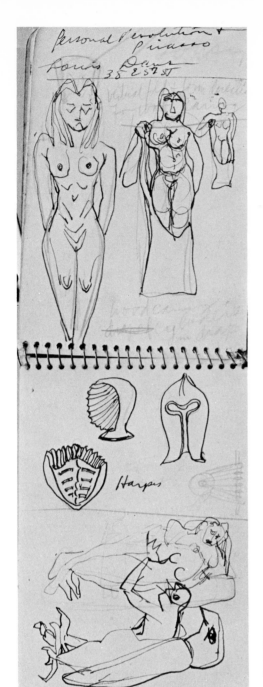

88
Page from Notebook #12. Early 1940s. Archive III/604.
89
Page from Notebook #10. Early 1940s. Archive III/580.

90
Canopic Head. 1951.
Steel, 42½ × 33 ×
155⅛ inches. Estate of
the artist.

91
Albany V. 1959. Steel, painted black, 22⅛ × 19¾ × 24⅜ inches. Private collection.
92
Circles and Arcs. 1961. Steel, painted white, green, and blue, 75 × 37¾ inches. Estate of the artist.

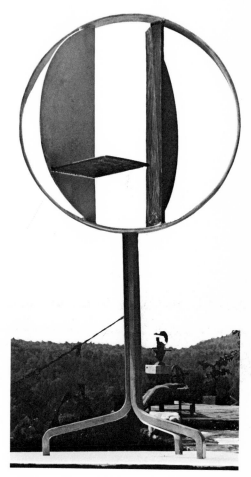

scan his work for the brute recurrence of certain thematic material is to be left with nothing but an endless litany of characterological difficulties and irrelevant private preoccupations. The possibility that nags at me while launching a discussion of the imagery is that the level of seriousness on which Smith reexamined the formal assumptions of contemporary sculpture might be missed, that I might end by making the sculptural product of his inquiry banal. But to ignore all the material that might help characterize Smith's formal intentions would be just as damaging to a real understanding of the sculpture. For without this information Smith's work is either seen as evidence of his vassalage to successive art-historical styles—first an apprenticeship to Cubist rhetoric, then an initiation into Surrealist incantation, and subsequently a vocation within the developing language of one branch of American painting[57]—or else individual works become the diagrammatic, bloodless solutions to problems posed almost at random.[58]

In pointing to the fact that the first two sculptures in the series of *Cubis*—the hieratic figure of *Cube III* (Fig. 93) and the female presence of *Cubetotem* (Fig. 94)—take up the formal themes of the *Tanktotems*, I am not trying to anthropomorphize the late work. Rather, by establishing the relation between the *Cubis* and the *Tanktotems*,

[57] In addition to the material by Kramer already cited (Introduction, p. 3; Chapter 1, fn. 22), one constantly reads remarks like "The ongoing development of Smith's work . . . bears a tangential but crucial relationship to the development of abstract painting in this country during the past twenty years" (Jane Harrison Cone, "David Smith," *Artforum* 5 [Summer 1967]: 73) or "The extent to which Smith's thinking was then dominated by prototypes of Abstract-Expressionist painting is clear from the singular form which much of his work of the late '40s and early '50s assumes" (Sheldon Nodelman, "David Smith," *Art News* 6 [February 1969]: 56). Either these critical remarks are totally empty or they must be given real content. Cone and Nodelman try to do this when they characterize Smith's formal development as one in which the problem of the framing edge—a problem peculiar to American painting of the 1960s—was constantly before him. Sections of this chapter are addressed to this question (pp. 79–90) and what its limitations are for understanding Smith's sculpture. See also pp. 153–170.

[58] "The formal and technical innovations that Smith made should first and foremost be seen as stemming directly, often haphazardly, from this absolute integrity to feeling." (Jane Harrison Cone, *David Smith* [Cambridge, Mass.: Fogg Museum, 1966], p. 2.) The problems she treats are: the relation of a cubist-derived composition to its frame; the problem of the base of a sculpture; and the question of color.

93
Cube III. 1961. Stain-
less steel, 95¾ × 33
× 19 inches. Estate of
the artist.

94
Cube Totem. 1961.
Stainless steel, 123½
× 90½ × 22 inches.
Estate of the artist.

I hope to provide a way of testing certain characterizations of the series as a whole, for I would like to show that it is irrelevant to see the *Cubis* as architectural in nature or to speak of them as Impressionist objects whose surfaces are invaded by and fuse with the atmosphere that surrounds them.[59] In addition, the acknowledgment of the relation between the two series might also prompt the realization that the *Cubis'* quality of detached surfaceness, which seems to radiate from the splayed frontality guaranteed by the fixed viewing point, did not result from a range of choices open to Smith from which he arbitrarily picked this or that one. Once he had assumed the burden of achieving sculptural presence, Smith's formal decisions became the self-generated directives of a quest.

[59] This position is taken by Jane Harrison Cone (ibid., p. 9): "The burnished, glinting surfaces of his stainless steel *Cubi* series had the effect of fusing each massive form with the air about it. Light caught and reflected over the fractured opacity of the surfaces seemed to dissolve the precise outlines of each form and drain the sculptures of their inescapable weightiness," and a slightly different one by Hilton Kramer (*David Smith* [Los Angeles: Los Angeles County Art Museum, 1966], p. 6): ". . . at certain moments it seems as if these sculptures were actually constructions of light itself, not so much occupying as illuminating the space that contains them."

Chapter Three   **Denial of Possession**

The Values of Surrealism

Drawing with the Found Object

If David Smith's career vibrates with the emotional tone of a battle campaign, this is at least partly justified. Smith was looking for formal alternatives to the whole of twentieth-century sculpture, and his ambition would allow him to stop at nothing less than a complete restructuring of the relation between the solitary work of art and its viewers. The character this career takes on is one of a quest, one that committed itself, moreover, to a kind of total originality. Paradoxically, the very recognition of Smith's self-imposed demands raises certain obstacles for a historical understanding of Smith's art, for it implies that one cannot necessarily see Smith's work in terms of a range of beliefs shared with his contemporaries, that his historical situation reveals less about his membership within a community of ideas than it does about his revolt from it. In short, it implies that the meaning of Smith's work must be sought outside the limits of a theory of style. This may seem puzzling in the case of David Smith, who, more than almost any other American painter or sculptor, has appeared to his critics to have predicated his work first on the transformations of European art that preceded his own development, and then on the dominant styles of American abstract painting.[1]

At the outset I maintained that Smith confronted the formal—and ultimately ideological—convictions of Cubist and Constructivist sculpture and launched his art on a course of conscious opposition. However, one could argue that Smith was not alone in opposing the Cubist-Constructivist entente. Surrealism, which dominated the thirties and forties like a glittering and eccentric diva, also turned its back on those formal ideals. Smith's knowledge of Surrealism can be amply documented, whether at the trivial level of his occasional biomorphism or at the deeper, more critical level of a formal language that depended on found objects and addressed itself to the idea of the totem. Is this double correspondence between the two vocabularies to be taken as proof of Smith's voluntary indenture to the premises and practices of Surrealism, or is it, like circumstantial evidence, a piece of behavior whose meaning is unclear without some way of reading the intentions that lay behind it? This question, prompted by his work of the forties, becomes particularly pressing when the totem image gains importance

[1] See Introduction, p. 3, and Chapter 2, pp. 105–116.

95
Lawrence Vail.
Bottle. 1944. Mixed
media, 16¼ inches.
Collection Yvonne
Hagen, New York.
96
René Magritte.
Bottle. 1959. Painted
bottle, 11¾ inches.
Collection Harry
Torczyner, New York.

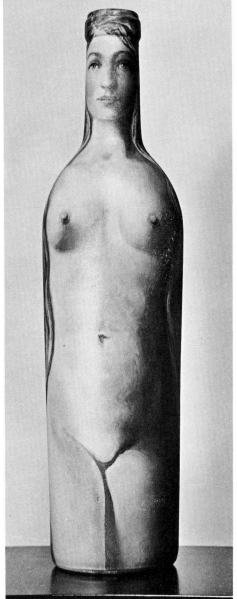

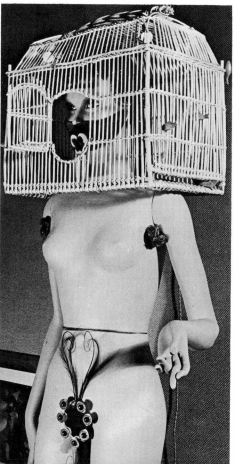

97
Salvador Dali. *The Venus de Milo of the Drawers*. 1936. Painted bronze, 39⅜ inches. Galerie du Dragon, Paris.
98
André Masson. *Mannequin*. Installed at the international exhibition of Surrealism in 1936.

in the sculpture of Smith's maturity. To answer it involves not only an examination of the documents surrounding Smith's art but a careful assessment of the meaning of Surrealism itself.

The Values
of Surrealism

During the forties, Smith was not the only American artist with an interest in the totem. In 1945, Jackson Pollock titled two narrow, vertical canvases *Totem I* and *Totem II,* and the names of other works of the same time referred obliquely to this theme (for example, *Night Ceremony, Moon Woman Cuts the Circle*). Among the better-known sculptors only Seymour Lipton actually constructed a specific totem (1957), although the titles of pieces produced by Herbert Ferber and David Hare during the 1940s invoke ideas of occultism and magic. It might therefore seem a violation of the rule of Occam's razor to examine Smith's biography and to speculate about his motives in order to explain the role that the totem image played in the growth of his style. In this case, what seems the least complicated and most direct explanation would simply tempt one to add Smith's artistic voice to the chorus of American painters and sculptors who are generally seen as accompanying the birth and early growth of Abstract Expressionism with a Surrealist-derived litany of mystical, unconscious revelation.

The presence of Surrealism in any art object of the forties or fifties purporting to be advanced has by now almost become a test of its authenticity. So unshakable is the faith that Surrealism was fundamental to the growth of American postwar painting and sculpture that the first two-thirds of Smith's career is always examined in terms of the role one or another aspect of Surrealism played in shaping his mature sculpture.[2] At first there seems to be plenty of evidence for this approach. After all, the corpus of his art during the 1940s is filled with the phantom dream territories of the "landscapes," the apparitions of the "spectres," and finally the appearance of the "totems." Was it not a tenet of Surrealism that art should "give form to the anatomy of intangible reality—the substance of feelings, of automatic responses and associations, dreams, totem,

[2] See Chapter 2, fn. 57.

myth, and fable, of the intimate nature of things and the nature of the intimate relations of things"?[3] What is the meaning of the morphological relation between some of
the forms Smith used in the mid-forties and those of Ernst, Tanguy, and the Boisgeloup
Picasso,[4] if it does not attest to Smith's journey toward the irrational as a source of
creative power? And finally there is his so-called acceptance of automatism in the early
fifties, with its attendant incorporation of ready-made and found objects into the body
of the sculpture. Is this not all irrefutable evidence for Smith's dependence upon the
Surrealist experiment?

Yet the fact of a shared image or body of images does not in itself explain
anything more about Smith's art than, say, the fact that van Gogh in his portraits
of empty chairs and cast-off shoes drew on the body of images common to the
sentimental calendar art of the Second Empire. In the case of van Gogh, there has
never really been a confusion between the meaning of the source and the meaning
of the image as it finally appears in his canvases. This may be due both to the low
esteem we have for popular imagery and to the strength of the van Gogh legend, which
interposes his personality somewhere between us and the work. It is like a sentinel,
reminding us of the powerful transformations to which sentimental themes of hope or
despair had to submit. But this clear separation no longer seems to be present in the
historical picture of the symbiosis between modern American art and the contemporaneous European movements we most esteem. The commonly held picture of Smith
during the forties and early fifties as a Surrealist-influenced sculptor is not therefore
neutral but has its own meaning, in that it tends to imply both shared values and
shared attitudes toward form, involving not only for Smith's work during the forties,
but his entire career. Thus, in denying the picture of Smith as a participant in the Surrealist experiment, two issues need to be examined—the first is formal; the second,
moral.

In the first two chapters of this book, when I spoke of Smith's rejection of the central

[3] See *First Papers of Surrealism* (New York: Coordinating Council of French Relief Societies, 1942).
[4] See Chapter 2, fn. 36.

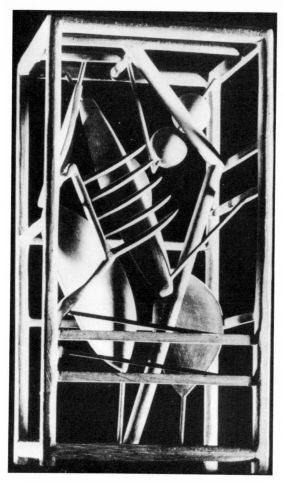

99
Roland Penrose. *The Last Voyage of Captain Cook.* 1936-1967. Mixed media, 27 × 26 × 34 inches. Collection of the artist.
100
Alberto Giacometti. *Cage.* 1931. Wood, 30 inches. Moderna Museet, Stockholm.

spine that makes sculpture intellectually possessable, I tried to set out the absolute formal distinction between Smith's sculpture and Surrealism. I said that the projection of objects in terms of such a spine or core was characteristic not only of Cubist-derived and Constructivist sculpture but of Surrealist work as well. Whereas the Constructivist core addressed itself to the possibility of absolute knowledge and judgment—the idea that there is a discoverable and correct shape for every geometrical figure—the Surrealist core posited knowledge without judgment: the essence of the object is knowable but ineffable.

The standard repertory of Surrealist sculptural forms involved cages in which objects were mysteriously trapped, hollow objects with empty cores (like the bottles of Magritte or the pierced forms of Moore, Hepworth, and Arp), or skeletal structures often tremendously bloated to become themselves volumes or containers for some more interior secret presence. All of this symbolism for holding, containing, trapping, enclosing is ultimately a set of metaphors for possession, and possession was at the heart of the Surrealist view of objects. Seeing each object as the locus of unconscious desires, Breton regarded the presence of the object as a provocation of the will to possess and ultimately to violate, or what one writer has termed "Surrealism's basic belief in the omnipotence of desire."[5] For Breton the first principle of beauty was to be the convulsive quality of *érotique voilé:* "provoking in the spectator a physical sensation that differs from erotic pleasure in degree only."[6] Because one happened upon it by chance, and because it could satisfy the compulsion to possess, the *objet trouvé* was for Breton the supreme expression of the Surrealist law, "To each according to his desire."[7] Compressed into that little aphorism is the bond that Surrealism programmatically

[5] Clifford Browder, *André Breton: Arbiter of Surrealism* (Geneva: Droz, 1967), p. 61.
[6] See *L'Amour fou* (Paris: Gallimard, 1937), pp. 12-26.
[7] André Breton, *Entretiens* (Paris: Gallimard, 1952), p. 264. Breton says in 1948: "Il est bien certain qu'aux célèbres 'à chacun selon ses capacités,' 'ses oeuvres' ou 'ses besoins' (matériels), non seulement le surréalisme mais toute la poésie digne de ce nom tend à substituer un 'à chacun selon ses désirs.'"

101
Spectre of War. 1944.
Steel, painted black,
11¼ × 6 × 22 inches.
Collection Mr. and
Mrs. Jan de Graff,
Portland, Oregon.

forged between the image of possession and the idea of a total laissez faire. It is to
Smith's analysis and condemnation of this attitude that I would like now to turn.

It must be fairly clear by now that Smith mustered his entire sculptural power against
possession. His substitution of surface for core as the primary datum of the sculpture,
his refusal to draw, his insistence on illusion: all speak of his will to defeat possession.
But these aspects of his work do not really become ascendant until the early 1950s.
And it is the work of the 1940s that is insistently characterized as Surrealist. What of
the 1945 spectres and bronze figures or the 1946 landscapes?

Of the five spectres executed during the 1940s, four of them are directly addressed—
at least in part—to Smith's political convictions and to the war. The political message
of *Spectre of War* (Fig. 101), *Jurassic Bird* (Fig. 102), *False Peace Spectre* (Fig. 103), and
Spectre of Profit (Race for Survival) (Fig. 104) is quite simple and direct. Smith accepts
an analysis of the war, with its senseless brutality and victimization, as the capitalist
solution to the problem of man's survival as a species. As Smith himself noted, with
regard to *Spectre of Profit,* for the "capitalist conception of man—war [becomes the]
natural condition of selection." And in that sculpture the image he uses to portray
the strong devouring the weak is one of "tied people carried in a spoon," held in the
mechanical paws of the spectre.[8] Elsewhere, next to notations of books like *Biology
and Marxism,* he writes, "It is the dialectic of survival."[9]

As in his earlier *Medals for Dishonor,* a persistent feature of the spectres is the
cannon/phallus as a symbol of violation. But these works, with their tone of overt
Marxism, widen the question of war to include the viciousness of class struggle. The
word "spectre" has less to do with the dream phantoms of Surrealism than with an
ironic play on Marx's image, in the *Communist Manifesto,* of the spectre of Communism
haunting Europe. This is not to say that these works operate only on a didactic level,
removed from impulses and motives Smith could recognize as his own. As always,
the cannon operates as a mask for Smith himself, acknowledging his own capacity for

[8] See Archive III/880.
[9] Archive III/937.

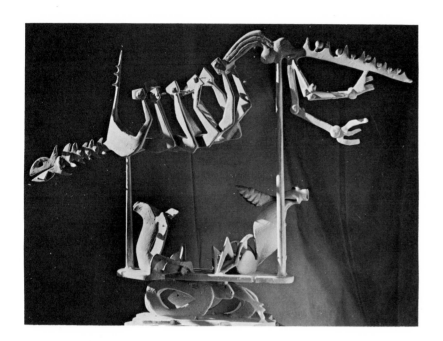

102
Jurassic Bird. 1945.
Steel, painted white,
25⅜ × 35½ × 7¼
inches. Collection Dr.
and Mrs. Paul T.
Makler, Philadelphia.

103
False Peace Spectre.
1945. Bronze and steel,
painted blue, 12½ ×
27¼ × 10¾ inches.
Collection Dr. and
Mrs. Ralph Jessar,
Philadelphia.

violence. Thus, in the construction of these sculptures there are overtones of a *mea culpa,* for Smith uses detail, much of it sensual, to arrest the viewer's attention and to slow down the pace of perception by fragmenting the forms and working against the grain of the thrusting gestures of the sculptures. On the peculiar level of delectation this provokes, the spectres are reminiscent of Goya's *Disasters of War* and what the late nineteenth-century critic Elie Faure wrote of them: "One cannot deny that a constant sadism prevails, that Goya takes pleasure in display amidst the odour of corpses and blood, the bellies of women . . . their fleshy thighs, their pointed breasts and beautiful, opulent necks and thrown-back chins." Sharp contrasts of light and dark pick out details of mutilation and violence that harrow the viewer with the realization that Goya's "righteous anger is mingled with and perhaps even augmented by sensuality."[10] In the same way, in Smith's *Spectres,* the cannon/birds seem to fuse terror with eroticism. If the violence portrayed in the spectres is applicable to the artist as well as to others, it is to that extent doubly moral. It involves not only an analysis of an external, political situation, but also a self-revelation whose meaning is insistently ethical in character. The recognition of guilt leads in Smith's work to the prohibition against touching, to the institution of the act of seeing countered by an act of self-knowledge that is moral in kind. This is the role of the totemic image within Smith's later sculpture, and, with regard to Surrealism, it is significant that Smith followed Freud and not Breton in his interpretation of the totem. Lévi-Strauss, whose disagreement with Breton's interpretation of totemism was published in *L'Art magique,*[11] characterized totemism as a primitive morality rather than, as Breton saw it, the ritualized confusion of desire with reality.

Although the argument between Lévi-Strauss and Breton over the meaning of totemism may seem like a minor issue, it really touches on the doctrine of Surrealism, which became increasingly specious and repugnant to Breton's contemporaries. In

[10] Elie Faure, *The Disasters of War* (New York: Phaidon Press, 1937), p. 10.
[11] André Breton, *L'Art magique* (Paris: Formes et Reflets, 1957). Lévi-Strauss's objections appear in the section entitled "Enquête," p. 56.

104
Spectre of Profit (Race for Survival). 1946. Steel and stainless steel, 18⅜ × 33½ × 6¼ inches. Collection Mr. and Mrs. Nathan Allen, Greenwich, Connecticut.

doing so, it puts pressure on one of the central arguments of the movement: the nature of the surreal itself. To Breton it was a primordial coherence that existed before a puritanical Reason was erected to institute false distinctions between good and evil, perception and idea, reality and desire. Breton's need for proof that such a coherence had existed, exists, and in the future could exist for everyone led him to claim a precedent for the surreal in the totemic and fetishistic practices of primitive cultures and in what he thought was the absolute confusion between subjective and objective experience in the hallucinations of the insane. Just as Lévi-Strauss could show that Breton seriously misinterpreted anthropological material in his search for the surreal, perceptual psychologists could demonstrate that the notion that mental patients cannot perceive the difference between hallucination and reality is also a fiction.[12] So on a factual level Breton's instances of the surreal are suspect. But it was against the moral implications of the surreal that the major attack came. For the surreal posits a level of experience that is "outside of all aesthetic or moral preoccupations," and indeed that very phrase was the one the *First Surrealist Manifesto* used to define Surrealist behavior itself. As early as 1925, Naville characterized the movement as anti-Marxist and as a self-indulgent adventure that was fundamentally antirevolutionary. Under the pressure of the Communist party's hostility to Surrealism throughout the 1920s, Breton shifted his definition of Surrealism to behavior "outside of all *conscious* preoccupations." But this was simply conjuring with words, since Breton saw the unconscious as the seat of irrational and amoral forces: it was the realm of the uncontrolled and cannibalistic primitive id. The charges of immoral escapism were leveled again and again during the thirties and forties until in *Qu'est-ce que la littérature?* the impressive voice of Sartre spelled out the rules according to which Surrealism had defaulted into an escape from freedom.[13]

[12] See Maurice Merleau-Ponty, *The Phenomenology of Perception* (London: Routledge and Kegan Paul, 1962), pp. 334 ff.
[13] This argument is made throughout *Qu'est-ce que la littérature?* first published in 1947, translated into English as *What Is Literature?* (New York: Harper & Row, 1965), pp. 185 ff. See particularly the chapter called "The Situation of the Writer in 1947."

There was no way for Breton to reconcile his own systematic confounding of
the powers of consciousness with the Marxist demand for analysis; in the eyes of Sartre,
for whom freedom implied responsibility for one's actions, he was seen as guilty. It
could of course be argued that Breton had indeed proceeded toward self-analysis in
works like *Les Vases communicantes* and *L'Amour fou*, where the author combed
through dreams, automatic texts, and waking experience, analyzing them for their autobiographical and prophetic meaning. Thus, though analysis was not an evident characteristic of Surrealist art as a whole, Breton himself employed it. But within the context
of Surrealism analysis was totally gratuitous. Analysis simply became a prod for driving
the unconscious to further, more elaborate gestures of possession, prolonging the vaga-
bond search for objects of desire. (The image of this quest held by many of his
contemporaries was one of Breton restlessly roaming the streets of Paris in the hope
that chance would present him with an object of love. Founded on the principle of
the insatiability of desire, Breton's view of action was like the endless chain of copu-
lation in a pornographic novel, which can never really reach a climax and can never
refocus consciousness on the self.)[14]

It may have been that David Smith's political commitment to Marxism in the late
1930s and early 1940s helped him come to a critical assessment of Surrealism. I have
also been suggesting that the perspective Smith maintained on his own impulses toward
brutal sexuality made the unanalyzed propositions of Surrealism something he felt
compelled to grapple with. But whatever we accept as the cause, his work of the
forties undeniably mounts an attack on the basic premises of Surrealism. On the one
hand, as we shall see in the landscapes, there is a search for alternatives; on the other,
a need to conduct exactly the kind of analysis of Surrealist sculpture that its practi-
tioners and advocates consistently avoided. Thus in the two sculptures of 1945, where,
at first glance, Smith seems most absorbed with both the motives and syntax of Sur-

[14] In "Art and Objecthood," Michael Fried compares Surrealism's emphasis on temporality with
Minimal Art's insistence on inexhaustibility—on an experience of the sculpture in terms of duration. *Artforum* 5 (Summer 1967): 23, fn. 18.

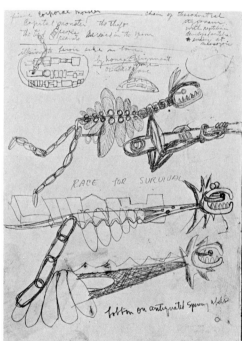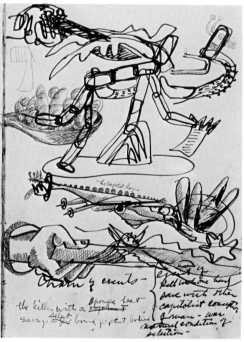

107
Reliquary House.
1945. Bronze and steel
painted black, 12½ ×
25½ × 11¾ inches.
Collection Mr. and
Mrs. David Mirvish.

realist art, his intention in fact seems to entail a laying bare of the Surrealist attitude toward objects.

This is done in *Reliquary House* (Fig. 107) by taking up the idea of the cage or container of the object and making it explicit. Having copied the work's structure from an illustrated diagram of a reliquary chest (see Fig. 108), Smith executes it in cast iron, accentuating the difference between the rigidity and flatness of the container and the shiny, voluptuous quality of the bronze objects or relics that it holds. Furthermore, the relics themselves are as idiomatically distinct from one another, from the point of view of style, as they are physically separate within the visible compartments of the container. Each one is in fact an individual relic of Smith's history as an artist,[15] and the

[15] The structure of *Reliquary House* was adapted by David Smith from a diagram of a reliquary chest that he had taken from a book and pasted into one of his sketchbooks (III/828). On the published diagram he drew elements that appear in the finished sculpture: a series of biomorphic shapes on the shelf of the box, reminiscent of a recumbent figure; above it a schematically drawn moon with rays extending from it and eyes attached to the rays (in the manner of the Egyptian Tel el Amarna depiction of the sun). Next to the drawing Smith scribbled, "shrine/repository for relics"; above it, "domestic reliquary." (See Fig. 108.) Another notation on a drawing that relates to this sketch indicates that the home to which Smith is referring is that of his childhood, for he writes, "a bundle of neat little sticks (soap opera tears and frayed ends/a mechanical pile of cut and drys, the pies of mother/the bromides of father)." (See IV/646.)
Like *Pillar of Sunday* (see Chapter 2, fn. 46), then, the sculpture seems to be about Smith's protest against the conventionality of his family. Yet it is more complicated than that. On a different page of the sketchbook (Fig. 109), Smith redraws the moon with eyes, labeling it "Influence of the moon on women's minds." (The *specific* source for the moon with eyes is a seventeenth-century engraving by an unknown artist, titled *L'influence de la lune sur la teste des femmes.* It was reproduced in *Verve* 1, no. 4 [1939]: 61. My attention was called to this by Edward Fry. On the facing page is another engraving by a sixteenth-century artist, Jean de Lery, showing nude women outside a stockade torturing two men. [See Figs. 110 and 111.] The *Verve* article generally deals with images of female cruelty and abandon.) This page (Fig. 109) is filled with voluptuously drawn nudes juxtaposed to the cannon/phallus image. In the context of Smith's other drawings and erotically "corrected" magazine photographs of women at play in a kind of wanton abandon (see Fig. 113), the implication of the drawing seems to be that women are uncontrollably sensual, the personification of *luxuria,* a tribe of maenads. Thus the presence of the moon image in the finished sculpture, added to the

108
Page from Sketchbook
#23. 1933–1945.
Archive III/828.
109
Page from Sketchbook
#23. 1933–1945.
Archive III/840.

110
Illustration in *Verve* 1,
no. 4 (1939): 61.
"L'Influence de la lune
sur la teste des
femmes." 17th cen-
tury. (This volume is
in Smith's library in
Bolton Landing. See
Fig. 109.)
111
Page in *Verve*
facing Fig. 110. Jean
de Lery and Théodore
de Bry. 16th century.
(See Figs. 46 and
112.)

whole ensemble reverses the formula of Surrealist cage/container sculpture. Where Giacometti, for example, strives for stylistic uniformity between the interior objects and their exterior shell (see Fig. 100), Smith stressed disparity. Giacometti's purpose is twofold: to give the composite the mysterious visual coherence and plausibility of dream objects, and to secure the logical relationship between the interior elements or "essence" of the work and its volumetric exterior. Giacometti's content is still the imperialist metaphor of the cage or trap, addressing itself to the arbitrariness, almost the wantonness, of the sculptor's will to possess. The objects appear to the artist from outside his life and are colonized into a rigid order by his desire. But in *Reliquary House* Smith seems to be purposefully maintaining a kind of stylistic heterogeneity; the relation of one part of the work to another is not imposed but comes from the unity of his lived experience. It is as though his life entailed those emblems. Smith liked to speak of his kinship to James Joyce. If there is such a relation, then it is between the kind of logic sought by the images in *Reliquary House* and the way that Joyce's language games bring ideas together in an effort to uncover the necessary rela-

sensuously polished bronze figure reclining on the upper shelf of the structure, seems to contradict the idea of the house as a repository for repellent objects. Smith seems to be addressing himself to his own feelings of fascination with them, no matter how odious they might be. (This transformation becomes specific in two etchings Smith made in the early forties, where the *Verve* engraving of women inside the stockade is inverted to transform the penned-up nudes into victims of explicitly sadistic acts. See Figs. 46 and 112.)

In the finished sculpture, the moon with eyes appears at the ground level of the work, along with a sheaf of sticks or wheat. Although Smith identified these objects in the pages of the sketchbook referred to before, they also operate on another level. In 1943, Smith was commissioned by an agency called China Defense Supplies to create a medal to honor foreign service to the government of China. His sketches for this medallion concentrated on a sheaf of grain and an image of the sun. (See IV/21.) Therefore, the *Reliquary House* combines allusions to Smith's feelings about his early life with references to his very recent past: to his growing reputation as a sculptor. The other internal reference to Smith's career is found in the object on the right side of the sculpture. A truncated, fluted column that sprouts petals, in the center of which, like the stamen of a plant, is a half-length female nude, recalls both *Table Torso* (see Fig. 76) and the prostitute figure from the *Medals for Dishonor* series.

115
*Medal for Dishonor:
War Exempt Sons of
the Rich.* 1939–1940.
Bronze, 10½ × 9
inches. Estate of the
artist.

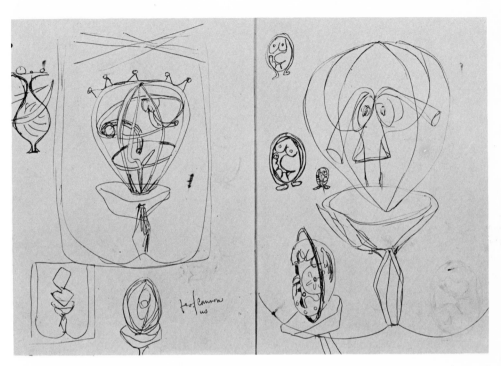

116
Page from Sketchbook
#41. 1944–1954.
Archive IV/88.

one of grafting-on, of arbitrariness, so that if the work has any meaning, it must be borne on the surface of the object.[17] These sculptures, like the *Spectres,* may imply a criticism of Surrealist ideology in both its visual and its thematic directions. But they do not really dismantle the basic formal premise that Surrealism shared with other modern sculpture at mid-century. Rather it is in the landscape series that began in 1945 and continued until 1951—often offered as evidence for Smith's absorption into the Surrealist symbology of dreamscape and fantasy—that one finds a concerted negation of Surrealism's first principles. In direct opposition to Breton's postulation of "desire as representation,"[18] Smith inaugurated a sculptural situation that would reveal desire as illusion.

Now, in sculpture, illusion does not raise, as it does in painting, the question of a third dimension that the painting does not really possess: a space into which we cannot actually enter. The sculpture is as real as our bodies and occupies space as they

letters that Smith used in this work and others from the same year (Fig. 56) were part of an assortment of junk metal Smith bought from a hardware dealer.

Smith also refers to Joyce in "The Language Is Image," *Arts and Architecture* 59 (February 1952): 20, and in his remarks in "Two Recent Purchases," *Brooklyn Museum Bulletin* 19 (September 1958): 13. The critic who dealt with this relation in the forties was Stanley Meltzoff ("David Smith and Social Surrealism," *Magazine of Art* [March 1946], pp. 98–99.)

[17] In a series of Smith's sketches from 1945 (Fig. 116), one can follow the transformation of the idea of a bottle or container of some kind into the hieratic form of the totem that wears its meaning on its surface. The sketches begin with enwombed-fetus images in the manner of *Growing Forms* (see Fig. 65) and move toward the cannon/phallus shape that obsessed Smith during these years. Some of the transitional images that closely resemble *Perfidious Albion* Smith labeled "small totems." In an article discussing the multileveled sexuality of Smith's work at this time, Stanley Meltzoff compared this work and *The Rape* (Fig. 51) to imagery from *Finnegans Wake.* Smith, who frequently referred to his interest in the *Wake* (see fn. 16), had even named his dog Finnegan. It is quite possible that Smith drew the title for this work from the pages of Joyce's book (see p. 343 in the 1939 edition, published by Faber and Faber). "Albion" is the nineteenth-century reference to England as an imperialist and victimizing industrialist power. In the *Medal for Dishonor: War Exempt Sons of the Rich* (Fig. 115), two female torsos that resemble *Perfidious Albion* weigh down the figures of a soldier and a welder, in a composite image of exploitation.

[18] In 1935 Aragon called for an end to "la sexualité comme système et le délire comme répresentation." (*Pour un réalisme socialiste,* quoted in Clifford Browder, *André Breton,* p. 127.)

do. The illusion in sculpture turns on the question of possession itself: either actual physical possession or, in a more sublimated form, intellectual possession—the viewer's ability to comprehend. The evidence amassed so far suggests the hypothesis that there were several levels on which Smith felt that to use a sculptural language to extol and convey possession was to contaminate it and to strip it of any possibility of being serious. Smith drew a parallel between his own destructiveness and the mass destructiveness of a capitalist society. The cannibalistic imagery of *Spectre of Profit* thus addresses to society as a whole what Smith saw as true for himself and others as individuals—that the image of a free man is not that of an amoebalike id moving over the face of the earth and extending pseudopodia of willfulness to engulf and incorporate the objects of desire. Freedom is instead unequivocably tied to the recognition of the autonomy and freedom of others. Because it is fundamentally tied to this deep sense of reciprocity, freedom itself depends on admitting that the willful realization of one's desires is an illusion of freedom, not, as Surrealism preached, the means to achieve it.

This was, then, the deepest level on which the fundamental opposition between the graspable, incorporable object of Surrealism and the formally distanced object created by Smith rested. If it is an opposition that is ultimately moral, then the fact that David Smith resolved *every* formal question that sculpture could pose with reference to it suggests what the stakes were in his implied criticism of the whole corpus of "modern" sculpture. We have already seen how this criticism operates in Smith's decision to adopt flatness or, what seems to me more exact, surfaceness, as his medium. We saw how the exvertebrate character of his objects dispelled as a false problem the issues raised by invertebrate sculpture with its implicit acceptance of the monolith. But the reason that Smith could reject the monolith so finally and so deeply was that lurking behind its every guise or shape he saw the issue of possession.

In the kind of sculpture that intends to convey to the viewer the title to its own possession, each of its successive faces acts as a variation on the object's underlying geometrical theme or shape. Whether we are talking about the carve-direct reference to the original block or about skeletal constructions, or about archetypally simpli-

117
Home of the Welder.
1945. Steel, 21 × 17⅜
× 14 inches. Estate of
the artist.

118a
Home of the Welder.
(alternate view)
118b
Home of the Welder.
(alternate view)

fied geometrical shapes, we see everywhere the sculptor's effort to make each aspect of the work transparent to every other. Shining through each facade of the object is the idea of the primal volume to which the surface at hand is only a particular or partial referent. Thus, whether the sculptor presents the prime volume physically, in its solid, blocklike objecthood, or conceptually, by laying bare its underlying structure, the key to making it seem possessable is to permit the viewer to sense the primal shape as a reality that lies behind any one particular view. Henry Moore fully articulates this when he describes the sculptor as someone who "gets the solid shape, as it were, inside his head—he thinks of it, whatever its size, as if he were holding it completely enclosed in the hollow of his hand. He mentally visualizes a complex form *from all round itself;* he identifies himself with its center of gravity, its mass, its weight; he realizes its volume, as the space that the shape displaces in the air."[19] It is not only in Moore's monolithic idealism but in the program of every major sculptural movement of the century that we can read the ambition to arm the viewer to capture and hold a sense of this "reality." Why then should we be surprised to hear, behind all the words of praise written in its behalf, the tone of pleasure taken in the heightened sense of possession that such sculpture worked to promote?[20]

[19] "Notes on Sculpture" (1937), reprinted in *Modern Artists on Art,* ed. Robert Herbert (Englewood Cliffs, N.J.: Prentice-Hall, 1965).
[20] Speaking of Moore's reclining figures, which are all expressly related to the original monolithic block from which they have been carved, Bowness says: "Once you are inside the sculpture, so to speak, all sorts of new formal and rhythmic possibilities are implied. . . . The sensation of being enclosed, as in a cave, gives rise to a whole series of associations, both prehistoric . . . and prenatal." (Alan Bowness, *Modern Sculpture* [New York: Dutton, 1965], p. 97.) Herbert Read goes further when he defines sculpture itself as "an art of palpation—an art that gives satisfaction in the touching and handling of objects. That, indeed, is the only way in which we can have direct sensation of the three-dimensional shape of an object." (*The Art of Sculpture* [New York: Pantheon, 1954], p. 48.) In 1932 Wilenski also had praised modern sculpture for being "microcosmic in formal character" and being able to generate imaginatively a sense of "universal scale." This notion of scale as an independent variable he compares to the experience of seeing sculptures in photographs, where "we instinctively assume the scale to be the one most appropriate to the form's significance." He goes on to say, "The more the meaning is 'caressability,' the more likely we are to assume from a photograph that the statue was of the size that can be easily handled and caressed." (R. L. Wilenski, *The Meaning of Modern Sculpture* [London: Faber and Faber, 1932], p. 161.)

One of the most important discoveries Smith made in the 1940s, during the course of his work on the landscapes, was that by directly confronting the fact that freestanding objects have successive aspects or faces, he could defeat the perception of the internally coherent volume and thereby the viewer's sense of possession. If the solid object's coherence is made possible only because every side refers to or stands in some sensible relationship to every other side, and all of them refer to or radiate out from a logical center or core, then this coherence can be subverted by making each facet of the sculpture radically different from the next. And this is what begins to happen in at least some of the landscapes of 1945–1946.

For example, if we compare the figurative relief carried on the front and back of the same major plane in *Home of the Welder* (Figs. 117 and 118), we find that these surfaces describe the same environment but do so on two entirely different scales. Therefore, as we move around the work, we do not have the same conviction that we have when looking at the four major views of an archaic kouros: the delineation of its surfaces all relate to the same body whose parts maintain the same scale relative to one another. Even though *Home of the Welder* approximates the simplest possible basic shape, a cube, Smith weakens our conviction that all of its faces belong to the same cube.

In *Landscape with Strata* (Figs. 119 and 120), Smith varies this technique slightly. Intersecting flat planes along the three coordinates of real space, he schematically displays the dimensions of height, width, and depth. The stereometry implied by this intersection is of course the primary tool of Constructivism's attempt to acquaint the observer both with the structure of space and with the objects that fill it. But in *Landscape with Strata* there is only *one* point of view from which the spectator can make sense out of the sculpture. From a point slightly left of the front of the work's base, the disparate planes suddenly fall into place: they suddenly cohere into an image of a bird flying through a dense area, perhaps the tops of trees. From any other point of view the sculpture seems capricious. The purity of the geometrical relation does not yield a heightened understanding of the dimensions of space,

119
Landscape with Strata.
1946. Steel, bronze,
and stainless steel,
16⅞ × 21 × 8½
inches. Estate of the
artist.

120
Landscape with Strata.
(alternate view)

because they are so far-flung and incoherent. Thus all we feel when we understand the sequence of their intersections is that this kind of geometrically coherent structure, far from making sense of the physical data, only renders them somehow arbitrary. We interpret distance in the work as we read it as an image: without regard to the actual size of the sculpture and the actual structure of it in our own three-dimensional space. In the grip of this illusion and the sense that it makes of the physical facts of the sculpture, it becomes irrelevant that from this point of view we have much less information about its physical structure—the real shape of the horizontal elements, for example, or the *real* distance from front to back of the work along the actual base. In the grip of a legible image, that is, there is no need for a conceptual grasp of the physical relation among elements in terms of the viewer's space.

Only by understanding this disjunction as the nature and substance of Smith's pictorialism can we see how different his solution was from that of the numerous other Americans like Callery and Lassaw who also in the 1940s began to explore painting as a resource for sculpture. The symptoms of their brand of pictorialism were fairly constant: the basic element of the sculpture became a flat and generally transparent plane that carried a sequence of linear imagery within its rectilinear frame. Generally there were three ways to assert this plane as sculpture. The first was simply to set it upon a base and present it as a kind of freestanding bas-relief. The second was to join several planes to form a space-enclosing box or volume. The third was to intersect several such freestanding pictures in stereometric, Constructivist terms.[21] Now, it seems to me

[21] In the early forties Harry Holtzman was taking the painting of Mondrian and materializing it as sculpture. Wrapping the opaque planes and black lines characteristic of Mondrian's paintings in the thirties around the four sides of a rectilinear column, Holtzman was drawing what was to him the logical consequence of a painterly statement from which all illusionism had been expelled. If Mondrian's canvases had become so flattened out that they confronted the viewer with a sense of themselves as objects, then the next step seemed to be to project them as the outer faces of a real, freestanding volume. The Holtzman sculpture pointed to the fact that in the absence of any pictorial illusion, spatial relationships between contiguous planes on the picture surface could only be carried out in real space on a surface that actually rather than fictively changed its direction with respect to the viewer. Thus Holtzman's assimilation of two- and three-dimensional media worked to materialize painting rather than to dematerialize sculpture. But this was unusual in American

121
Alexander Calder.
White Frame. 1934.
Wood panel, wire, and
sheet metal, 90 × 108
inches. Collection of
the artist.
122
Alexander Calder.
Thirteen Spines. 1940.
Sheet steel, rods, wire,
and aluminum, 84
inches. Collection of
the artist.

123
Ibram Lassaw. *Star Cradle.* 1949. Plastic and steel, 12 × 10 × 14 inches. Collection of the artist.

that far from representing a revolution in sculpture, the kind of pictorialism we find in such abundance in the 1940s is merely an attempt to use the inherent transparency of the picture plane to shore up what I have been pointing to as the ideals of traditional sculpture. The illusionist picture constructs from the *inside* the kind of spatial coherence and relatedness that must be carried by the normal sculptural object—like the kouros—on its exterior. It is characteristic of traditional painting that the figures arrayed along the plane facing the viewer carry, as the mark of their success as illusion, a clear implication of their position in space. Although the viewer looks at the painting as though he were part of an audience facing the proscenium of a stage, the inherent proposition of perspective is that the clarity of the picture's internal relationships should enable him to imagine the figures from all possible vantages. He should have access to them not only from the front but also from the side, feeling like a member of the audience and, simultaneously, like the director who stands in the wings and sees how the actors are ranged one behind the other. Thus in referring to the "box-space" of the illusionistic picture, I am pointing to the peculiar way that perspective projections describe depth as "breadth seen from the side."[22] The sculptor who seeks to mount intimations of its other three views on every face of the freestanding figure is striving for a similar conceptual lucidity. If the sculptor deserts the exterior articulation of the

sculpture of the forties; most of the other sculptors actively engaged in exploring the reciprocity between pictorial and plastic art were mining painting for the inherent transparency possessed by the picture surface, hoping to open their sculpture to a more insistent feeling of immateriality. Mary Callery's sculpture is a clear example of this, as is Lassaw's. The work of the latter is discussed in the text later, not because of its inherent interest but because of its relative importance for Smith. Lassaw seems to have been the one American whose sculpture influenced Smith in the 1930s (see Chapter 2, fn. 54). Another obvious example is Calder, who employs a picture frame this way throughout the thirties (see Fig. 121). With the mobiles, in the thirties and early forties, Calder relinquishes the frame and adopts the expressly skeletal idea of the European constructors (see Fig. 122). Calder's use of the spine is twofold: the slender wires expose the fibrous core of natural objects, and the eccentricity of their connection reveals that the internal coherence, the core running through the assemblage, is the natural equilibrium an object assumes with relation to gravity.

[22] See Merleau-Ponty, *Phenomenology of Perception,* p. 255

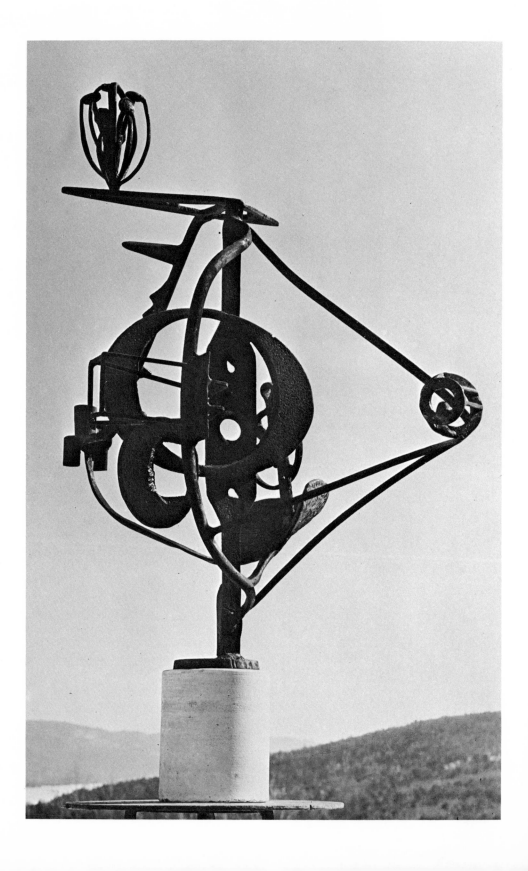

124
Blackburn: Song of an Irish Blacksmith. 1949–1950. Steel and bronze, 46¼ × 40¾ × 24 inches. Wilhelm Lehmbruch Museum, Duisberg, Germany.
125
Blackburn. (alternate view)

solid monolith and, like the Constructivist, examines the internal structure of the block stereometrically (see Fig. 10), then the intersected planes of his construction come even closer to the theoretical propositions of pictorial illusionism. The kind of pictorialism that entered American sculpture in the 1940s was therefore far from revolutionary. It was the natural extension of what I have been pointing to as the real tenor of twentieth-century sculpture: sculpture pervaded or infected by the Hildebrand perspective.

The work of Ibram Lassaw provides the most clear-cut example of this development. For example, in *Star Cradle* and the *Mandala* series (Fig. 123), Lassaw took rectangular planes and ornamented them with the imagery of current Abstract-Expressionist paintings, either by adding webs of enameled line to transparent planes of plexiglass or by torch-cutting ragged images out of milky surfaces of plastic. He intersected these planes at right angles, as in the 1949 *Star Cradle*, to offer the simple open cube of early Constructivism. Lassaw had faith in the internal consistency of this solution because he saw no contradiction between the innate transparency of the picture plane—through which one looked toward the ideal focus of vision—and the Constructivist notion of transparency. The Constructivist assumption had always been that the enterprise of making or looking at sculpture involved looking past the surface of an object toward its core, in order to grasp it in terms of an ideal geometry. Given this bias, Lassaw naturally wanted to stress the continuity between all the possible views one could have of any single sculpture. And since nothing could be more continuous than something that never changes, all the faces of one of these objects were absolutely identical.

If we compare Lassaw's *Star Cradle* and Smith's *Blackburn: Song of an Irish Blacksmith* (Figs. 124 and 125), we see the distance that separates Lassaw's quest for unity from Smith's arbitrariness and premeditated incoherence. In *Star Cradle* the principle of intersection establishes the core as a kind of generatrix for the planes that radiate out from it, like geometric emanations from an algebraic statement. Looking at *Star Cradle* from its "front," we are aware that if the work were to rotate on either its x-axis or its y-axis, it would continue to display the same information about this structure. But in *Blackburn,* where the structural principle is also one of intersecting planes or faces, Smith has deprived these planes of a sense of interrelatedness, obscuring any transparency between them. From one view *Blackburn* is all open silhouette. Small clusters of cotter pins and pipe section punctuate the joints of its hieratic torso. From this prospect *Blackburn* offers no resistance to the eye, which passes through the interior, reveling in an unparalleled sense of freedom. From another view *Blackburn* fans out in precarious balance across the viewer's plane of vision as irregular gesture. By moving ninety degrees around the work we have the powerful sense of seeing a different work, not merely a new aspect of *Blackburn.*

The arbitrary relation between one view of a sculpture and another became for Smith one more means of warding off possession. If it was used only tentatively in the early landscapes, by the end of his career it had become a blunt and effective weapon. Thus, in *Voltri XVII* (Figs. 126 and 127), we find a work whose front and side views, if seen only in photographs, would probably not be identified as belonging to the same sculpture. Head on, *Voltri XVII* appears to be an open frame raised on two legs. Four intersecting planes, visible only as edges, score the space inside the frame into a schematic grid. Above the frame one of the vertical lines of the grid has been turned ninety degrees to face the observer as a plumelike plane of metal. Taken as a whole, the work confronts the viewer with the flat head, the broad, square body, and the finely drawn legs of the totem image he has come to expect from Smith. What is more, the schematic geometry of the "torso" invites him to grasp this body by means of its apparent structural logic: there is something magnificently Doric about the work from this angle, as the heavy steel verticals rise to support the more massive lintel of the top of the frame, capped by the flangelike pediment above it. But this kind of comprehension is made utterly gratuitous by any other view of the sculpture. From the side, the interior vertical planes swell into two gently curving but unrelated shapes, neither one of which seems to support or be supported by the rest of the structure. Given the expectations raised by the front view of the work, we see in the profile an almost blowsy biomorphism, a swollen sensuousness that seems to come from nowhere. Or perhaps it would be more accurate to say that nothing else in the work would have seemed to guarantee its presence.

Voltri VIII (Figs. 128 and 129) shares with *Voltri XVII* both the conjunction of a rigidly hieratic front face with a voluptuously curvilinear profile and a lack of transparency between these two aspects of the sculpture—an opaqueness that has nothing to do with the actual openness or closedness of the object. With *Voltri VIII* there is once more no conceptual core to guarantee that the various views of the work will give a coherent impression. And it is this ambivalence that Smith continually forces the spectator to confront, much the way a Cubist painting constantly brings us up against the naked fact of the picture plane. In Cubism it is our very effort to coordinate the various segments of the depicted object, to adjudicate between the conflicting levels of implied space, that (in Greenberg's words) "undeceives the eye" and causes us to acknowledge the conflict between our expectations with regard to the painting and its utter material aloofness. The arbitrariness of *Voltri XVII* likewise confronts us with our efforts to rationalize the objects we see before us. In defeating our expectations and thereby upsetting our systems for the acquisition of knowledge and control, Smith analyzes for us our greatest illusion with regard to the sculptural object: the assumption that possession is the automatic correlative of desire.

Drawing with the Found Object

In looking from *Landscape with Strata* to *Blackburn* and *Voltri XVII*, I have traced the formation of a tactic by which a kind of parody of the monolith is used to attack its basic premises. The entirely flat, entirely frontal sculpture of works like *Hudson River Landscape* and *The Banquet* might seem to be a logical extension of this strategy, since nothing would seem to defeat the coherence of the three-dimensional object so much as a sculpture that tended to disappear as we moved around it. However, in the landscapes of the early fifties this is not the case. I have already said that as soon as Smith established a roughly rectangular format and drew in steel rod inside it, he found himself invoking the muse of painting, which was like opening the Pandora's

126
Voltri XVII. 1962. Steel, 95 × 31⅜ × 29¾ inches. Private collection.
127
Voltri XVII. (alternate view)

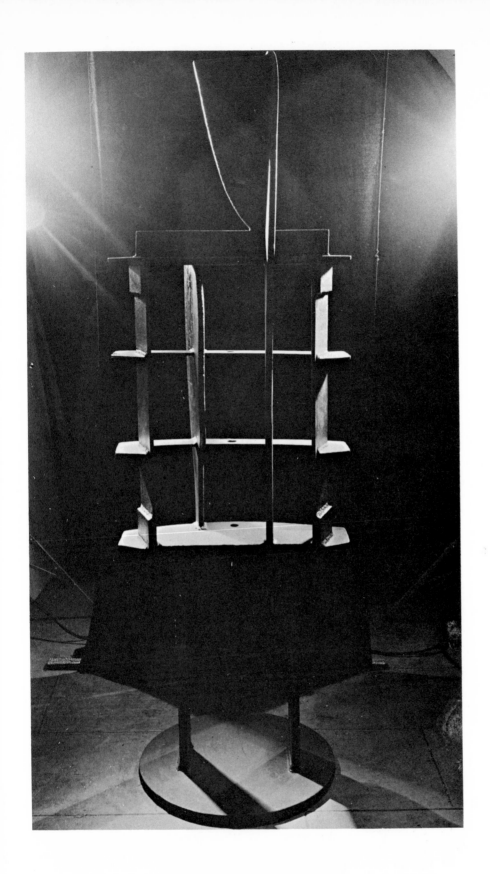

128
Voltri VIII. 1962. Steel,
79½ × 52½ × 33¾
inches. Estate of the
artist.
129
Voltri VIII. (alternate
view)

box of the traditional illusionist picture. Ironically, "drawing in space" simply affixed to steel line the same sense of vestigial weight and density that adheres to even the most stripped-down or schematic drawing as long as it appears within a traditional pictorial field. It seems fairly clear that this was why Smith stopped working with extruded and bent steel rods and, turning instead to the cursive shapes of tools and fragmented farm implements, began to "draw" with found objects. But right away he faced a new danger, for the found object was—rightly—one of the prime weapons in the Surrealist arsenal.

For Breton, the importance of the found object lay in its function as a metaphor for the way the solitary id incorporates and absorbs objects from the outside world. Dropped as though from nowhere into the stream of the finder's life, the object seemed able to form ripples of association and memory. Although by definition the object's discovery had to be fortuitous, at the same time it had to be a long time in preparation. One of Breton's favorite instances of the discovery of such an object was the spoon that he and Giacometti happened upon while at the Flea Market. The object's significance lay in the fact that it was not just any spoon: it was linked backward in time to the request for a particular sculpture that Breton had put to Giacometti several months before. It also recalled specific sexual fantasies Breton had about his future. Therefore in Breton's eyes it became uniquely *his* spoon, for his dream life and his past entitled him to it.[23]

Obviously the Surrealist sculptor could not operate on the assumption that objects that spoke with this kind of immediacy to his own unconscious needs and desires would elicit the same response in another viewer. In fact, the logic of Breton's thinking about the found object would pretty much guarantee that they could not. But the Surrealist sculptor could use the found object to simulate a sense of discovery and possession by introducing the object into the context of the viewer's already developed understanding of the human body and its structure. In this kind of sculpture, either the

[23] *L'Amour fou,* pp. 41–59. In 1936, in a review of the "Exposition d'objets surréalistes," Breton wrote, "Toute épave à portée de nos mains doit être considérée comme un précipité de notre désir." (Reprinted in Breton, *Le Surréalisme et la peinture* [Paris: Gallimard, 1965], p. 283.)

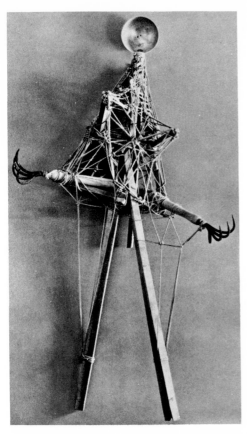

130
Picasso. *Personage.*
1935. Wood, string, and
metal, 44¾ × 24 × 14
inches. Collection of
the artist.
131
Picasso. *Baboon and
Young.* 1951. Bronze,
21 inches. Museum
of Modern Art, New
York. Solomon Gug-
genheim Fund.

132
Agricola VIII. 1952.
Steel and bronze,
painted brown, 31¾ ×
21½ × 18¾ inches.
Estate of the artist.

entire object becomes a visual pun on the shape of a human or animal body, or the object locates the pun in a section of the body: dinner forks serving as hands, household screws as claws, or a toy automobile as cranium. Whether the pun is to work upon the whole body or simply on its parts, the sculptor asks the viewer to take the resemblance for granted. Caught in the circular visual logic of found object as sculpture, the viewer often feels that he is witness to the very act of creation. Since the context is the structure of the body and its parts, the play with the found object is a play on the notion of representation. Its basic conventionality resides in the fact that it is simply an elaborately fanciful way of depicting a recognizable shape. (See Fig. 130.)

As long as the found object operates in the context of this game, it is unusable for Smith. The context is still another variation on the Hildebrand perspective. The game once more assumes that the viewer is omniscient, and the found object serves as the key to a transcendent reality which he is empowered to create as long as he continues to play the game.

In the early fifties, Smith was trying to maneuver within an extremely tight situation: he was caught between the pitfalls of drawing in space" and the natural allusiveness of the found object. As long as the intractably figurative quality of bent and extruded steel rods reads pictorially, it continues to point to a distinction between the inside and the outside of the object. On the other hand, almost any use of a found object tends to insist on a metaphorical relation to the structure of the human body, leaving nothing to the sculptor but the exploration of ever more imaginative depictions of it. In the grip of this representational mode, everything sculptural about the work becomes an ornamental overlay against the background of a conceptually familiar form.

Smith's response came in the series of nine *Agricolas*, which absorbed the major part of his energy in 1951 and 1952. Like his solution to the problem of transparency, Smith resolved the question of drawing through a programmatic arbitrariness. He began to use shapes—a combination of machine parts, dismantled tools, and forged steel rod—that bore no analogy to parts of the human anatomy. There were two major devices that he employed to deprive these shapes of the power to function as meta-

phors for a preconceived idea of the body. The first was to concentrate them at the outside edge of the sculpture, so that, as in the case of *Australia,* they could not be read as either forming a skeleton or issuing from a structural core. The second was to dismantle the tools so that the viewer could not interpret them as references to organic motion. This he did either by so fragmenting the machine elements or tools that their original function as tongs or calipers or wrenches was no longer legible, or by connecting them in such a way as to render their moving parts nonfunctional. Once dismantled, the tools unequivocally stated themselves as pure line, but only as a special form of line. Too segmented and disparate to function as a coherent, enclosing contour, the profiles of Smith's objects register only as the constituents of pictorial representation—as the emblems rather than the substance of depiction. The double edge formed by the two curved rods at the right side of *Agricola VIII* (Fig. 132) seems more like the parallel, hatched lines of calligraphic shading than the definitive contour of an object. The repetition of elipses along the top of *Agricola IX* (Fig. 134) reads like modeling for a volume that is otherwise absent. In *Agricola VII* (Fig. 133), the bunched and incoherent links of chain that comprise one side of the sculpture seem like patches of illusionistic shading rather than the firm outline of a depicted shape. Similarly, the ratchets of seven machine elements form the major visual event of *Tanktotem II* (Fig. 135) by surrounding the central disc of the boiler head with a sputtering corona of crosshatching. In the *Agricolas,* we see Smith continually stripping line of its power to designate a whole form and making it act instead as the disembodied device of pictorial illusionism.

 At the end of his life, Smith's use of the found object had not changed. Throughout the *Voltri–Bolton Landing* series he continued to stress its functional arbitrariness and to use it as a *means* toward depiction. In *Volton XVIII* (Fig. 137), for example, the heaviness of the metal sheet arching across its upper quadrant seems dissolved by the pictorial role it plays in the sculpture. As we look at the work, we see it not as a substantial contour but as a shadow cast by the phantom circle that paradoxically

133
Agricola VII. 1952.
Steel and cast iron,
painted red, 2⅞ ×
13⅞ × 9½ inches.
Collection Dr. and
Mrs. Richard Kaplan,
Philadelphia.
134
Agricola IX. 1952.
Steel, 36¼ × 55¼ ×
18 inches. Estate of
the artist.

135
Tanktotem II. 1952–
1953. Steel and bronze,
80½ × 49½ × 19
inches. Metropolitan
Museum of Art, New
York.
136
Voltri-Bolton X. 1962.
Steel, 81¼ × 42 ×
11¼ inches. Estate of
the artist.

137
Volton XVIII. 1963.
Steel, 110⅞ × 67⅛ ×
15⅛ inches. Anony-
mous collection.
138
Picasso. *Musical
Instrument.* 1914.
Painted wood, 24 ×
14½ inches. Collection
of the artist.

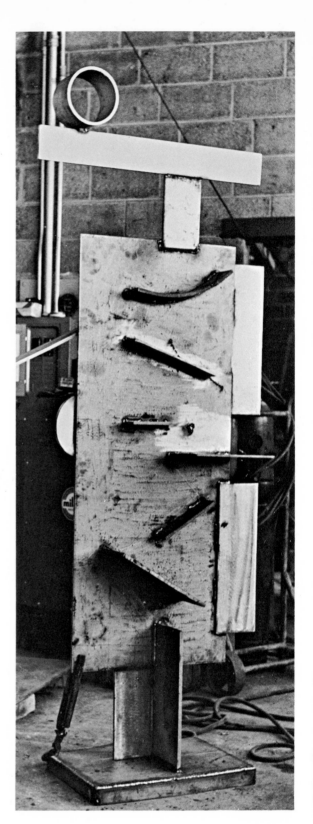

139
March Sentinel. 1961.
Stainless steel, 101¾
× 44 × 19¾ inches.
Collection Dr. and
Mrs. Paul T. Makler,
Philadelphia.
140
Two Circle Sentinel.
1961. Stainless steel,
86¼ × 53 × 27½
inches. Collection Mr.
and Mrs. Joseph
Iseman, New York.
(In this photograph
the work is not yet
finished.)

seems to occupy the sculpture's center. Thus, even while confronting the observer
with a newfound weight and massiveness in the over-life-size sculpture of this series,
Smith continued to absorb the found object into the pictorial language of illusion.

This transmutation of cast shadow has been seen before. In the constructions of 1914,
Picasso had wrenched cast shadow from the role it had played in earlier nineteenth-
century relief sculpture. Under his tutelage, shadows no longer gestured toward the
unknowable aspects of objects. Instead Picasso materialized them, treating them as a
kind of primary datum that was altogether known since it coincided completely with
the splayed surface of the construction. One of these objectified shadows—from
Musical Instrument (Fig. 138), a construction of 1914—strikingly resembles the
"shadow" in *Volton XVIII,* for it, too, is a rectangular sheet from which a circular fragment has been cut. In the Picasso, as in the Smith, this absent half-disc becomes the
major visual element of the work.

Picasso's absent shape reads as the ghost of a stringed instrument, perhaps a mandolin;
Smith's is completely abstract. This is not because Smith refers to a purely geometrical
shape rather than an object of sense experience. It it because Smith has moved his
point of reference back to the very conventions that make perception—and with it
meaning—possible: the convention of a ground against which meanings appear as in
relief. What becomes manifest for the first time in Smith's work is the perception that
this ground is something that all objects carry with them on their faces, not as an
"essence" buried at their hearts. In this piece the seamless coexistence of object
and meaning is visible and moving. The convention of relief—relief in its deepest
sense—finds its most abstract expression as it stands on its own without need of or
recourse to the backdrop of the actual ground plane that Picasso had still to employ
in 1914.

In his later work, when Smith occasionally reverts to a ground to set drawn
elements against, the sculptures seem both less radical and less successful. This happens in *March Sentinel* (Fig. 139) and *Two Circle Sentinel* (Fig. 140) from 1961. In both

cases the ground appears once again as a core from which the affixed figuration seems to grow. But if *March Sentinel* looks like conventional relief, it is only because of standards set by Smith himself elsewhere in his sculpture.

The two kinds of drawing that Smith explored in his mature work, drawing silhouetted against the support of a ground and the self-sustained drawing with found objects, unexpectedly coalesce in the last and, for many, the greatest phase of Smith's career. Huge stainless steel cubes, discs, cylinders, and bars come together to form the sculptures Smith called *Cubis*. Insofar as Smith regarded these tectonic elements as "found objects," they issue from his thinking in the *Agricolas* and the *Voltri–Bolton Landing* sculptures. Each face of each element supports a luminous calligraphy applied by Smith to the stainless surfaces with a carborundum disc. Although Smith was willing to concede that the color he applied to the surfaces of his earlier work was largely arbitrary and almost never really successful,[24] he was pleased with the burnishing on the *Cubis*. It is the one place in Smith's art where surface texture and what I have been calling surfaceness seem to coincide.

The *Cubis* not only culminate Smith's experience with drawing but also summarize and expand his thinking about the structural limitation of viewpoint between sculpture and observer. In that sense they feel like the grand *summa* of Smith's career—although clearly they were not meant by him to be its conclusion.

[24] In the Hess interview, Smith confessed, "I've only made two sculptures in tune properly between color and shape." This is the way the typescript now in the Smith Archive reads (IV/302); when the interview was published, the "only" was omitted. (See Bibliography, no. 58.)

141
Cubi XXVI. 1965.
Stainless steel, 119⅜
× 151¼ inches. Col-
lection Philip M.
Stern, Washington,
D.C.

No other series of Smith's has attracted as much attention from contemporary sculptors and critics as the *Cubis,* and yet no other series has elicited such diverse and mutually contradictory interpretation. Some writers treat the *Cubis* as abstract gestures or rhythms—as allusions to the stretching, striding, turning movements of a heroically scaled figure (Fig. 141). Others, moving with striking symmetry to the opposite point of view, think of them as colossal constructions—the first wave of sculpture's migration into the realm of architecture (Fig. 142). Those in the first group generally describe their formal experience of the works as colored by a sense of antimateriality; they speak of the illustion of masslessness and weightlessness, of light so captured and reflected that the sculptures dissolve into "dazzling emblems" and create "an energy that is purely optical."[1] As we would expect, the second group's perception of the works is the absolute reverse of this. For them the excitement of the *Cubis* resides in the unalloyed massiveness of the individual elements, in the sculptures' presentation of corporealized solid geometries. Representing this second position, the critic-sculptor Donald Judd described *Cubi XIX* (Fig. 143) as an inventory of shapes that are also objects.[2] Because each massive box or drum or beam presented its front face to him as a huge plane or an enormously thickened line, Judd saw the work as a drawing. Yet the elements of the drawing were irrevocably attached to declarative, three-dimensional volumes. Judd's satisfaction in the work issued from his sense of it as drawing wrenched off the page and congealed into a freestanding object. He saw it as drawing rescued from its customary hell of ambiguous pictorial illusionism and liberated into an unambivalent existence as an object. In this way, all of the questions one normally has about the spatial positions of any plane could suddenly and absolutely be resolved. In his eyes, *Cubi XIX* became, at one and the same time, the apotheosis and the defeat of the drawing tradition: the apotheosis because drawing was pushed to its logical conclusion and the defeat because such a conclusion "gets rid of the problem of illu-

---

[1] Hilton Kramer, *David Smith* (Los Angeles: Los Angeles County Museum of Art, 1966), p. 7.
[2] Exhibition review in *Arts* 39 (December 1964): 62.

142
Cubi XXVII. 1965.
Stainless steel, 111⅜
× 87¾ × 34 inches.
Solomon Guggenheim
Museum, New York.

143
Cubi XIX. 1964. Stainless steel, 113⅛ × 21¾ × 20 inches. Tate Gallery, London.

144
Cubi XXIV. 1964. Stainless steel, 114½ × 84¼ × 28¼ inches. Carnegie Institute of Art, Pittsburgh, Pennsylvania.

sionism and of literal space, space in and around marks and colors—which is riddance of one of the salient and most objectionable relics of European art."[3]

I think it is accurate to see the Cubis as the culmination of Smith's experience with drawing in the fifties. The Cubis should be related to the whole question of drawing with found objects, for Smith thought geometrical entities were as much "found" elements as tongs or wheels or wrenches. (He said, speaking of the *Cubis,* that they all had "a basic geometric form that is already 'found.' . . . Are triangles, circles and spheres 'found'? They have always been there.")[4] Like the *Agricolas,* the *Tanktotems,* and the *Voltri–Bolton Landing* pieces, the *Cubis* are images drawn across a continuous plane. In them, lines seem to span the plane: *Cubis XXII* (Fig. 145) and *XXVI* (Fig. 141) share this feature with *Agricola IX;* in *Cubis XXIV* (Fig. 144) and *XXVII* (Fig. 142), shapes edge out toward an enclosing boundary, though they never seem really to define it; in *Volton XVIII* and *Cubi XII* (Fig. 146), a series of surrounding shapes throw into relief, like cast shadows, a tautly empty expanse of space. And like the drawing of the three earlier groups, the *Cubis'* drawing continues to allude to the totem figure, upright, hieratic, and aloof.

As in the case of the earlier sculpture, Smith raises again the question of possession, for both the added sensuousness of the burnished material[5] and the order and rationality of the shapes themselves, pointing as they do to the idea of an underlying geometric logic, tantalizingly hold out the promise of a comprehensible form. But here, as before, Smith interposes between the sculptural object and the viewer a sense of the work's elusiveness. Never so blatant as here, Smith's structural arbitrariness deprives the *Cubis* of the logic of weight and support, of skeletal cohesiveness or a coherent center of

---

[3] "Specific Objects," *Arts Yearbook* 8 (1965): 66.
[4] Interview with Thomas Hess, *David Smith* (Marlborough-Gerson Gallery, New York, October 1964).
[5] Smith liked the effect of the burnishing on the *Cubis;* it was one way to make color a real function of the surface. He said, "I made them and I polished them in such a way that on a dull day they take on a dull blue, or the color of the sky in the late afternoon sun, the glow, golden like the rays, the colors of nature" (ibid.). That is to say, he did not think of the polishing marks as calligraphy. Sometimes the burnishing was done by Smith himself; sometimes it was executed by Leon Pratt, Smith's assistant.

145
Cubi XXII. 1964. Stain-
less steel, 103¾ × 77¼
inches. Yale University
Art Gallery, New
Haven, Connecticut.

146
Cubi XII. 1963. Stainless
steel, 110¼ inches.
Joseph H. Hirshhorn
Collection, New York.

gravity,[6] of the sense of completeness that adheres to the depiction of familiar things. Combined with this collapse of a structural logic, the resolute frontality of the works makes it clear that no real knowledge of them will come from a change in the spectator's point of view; everything to be known is given, as in a drawing or painting, from the front. But it is also true that we continue to feel the planes that face us as the front surfaces of three-dimensional objects, so that never before has this enforced frontality seemed so in conflict with the apparent bulk of the sculptures, or indeed with the nature of sculpture itself.

Through this conflict we are made to feel the distinction between frontality as a property of objects and frontality as a convention. To apply the word "frontal" to objects is to point both to the limited nature of our view of objects and to the fact that objects themselves have multiple faces. Thus, as a property of objects in the world, frontality refers to one of the many possible aspects that any three-dimensional entity necessarily has. Just as we can have an aerial view or a side or back view of an object, we can have a front view of it.[7] For many objects in the world, there is no clear priority

[6] This disequilibrium runs directly counter to the way Calder made delicate balance the theme of his mobiles, as though equilibrium itself ran like a core through the center of the works. See Chapter 3, fn. 20.

[7] This consideration of sculpture and its faces or aspects was common in the late forties and early fifties, particularly among those critics who were waging war against the authoritarian claims of the carve-direct aesthetic. Thus in 1950 Sidney Geist wrote an article in *It Is* called "Pardon My Front"— and the "my" in his title did not refer to the viewer but to the object. Geist began the article by saying: "The issue of frontality in sculpture is inescapably linked to the frontality of the human being and to the fact that since earliest times the human figure, with emphasis on its attractive, unobstructed and undistorted (by twisting or bending) 'front', has been the preferred subject for sculpture. However, I do not propose to discuss the portrayal of the human form in sculpture, but rather the structural frontality of sculpture.

"The question of frontality, then, arises when we consider sculpture designed to be seen from one side. Such sculpture has two extreme cases: sculpture designed to be seen from several sides, and planar sculpture, which has, as it were, only one side."

Similarly, David Smith wrote in 1951, "I don't consider always that sculpture should be conceived/ viewed in the round. The front view of a person who is sufficiently interesting is often sufficient. The rear view incidental. . . ." (Archive IV/1206.)

147
Cubi I. 1963. Stainless
steel, 124 × 34½ ×
33½ inches. Detroit
Institute of Art.

among views. To speak of the front face of a cube is simply to differentiate among
its surfaces relative to our position; nothing about it gives preeminence to one or
another of its sides. But in certain objects, like buildings, there does seem to be a
hierarchy both of perspectives on them and of facades that they expose to view. In
some instances, the front may be established by function, in others by structural
determinants, in still others by a ritually assigned meaning. It is this last that begins
to differentiate the object according to convention. As a convention, frontality
becomes a way of delimiting or defining a discrete mode of experience. Within
painting, it operates to set definite limits on the way one can approach the canvas; by
ruling out the relevance of the fact that the painting, like any object, has a back or
sides, it sets the conditions that are normative for experiencing pictures. And by doing
so it inhibits other means one might have of knowing an object—such as moving
around it, walking through it, exploring it by touch, dissecting it, picking it up—making
sight the only appropriate mode of apprehension.

In sculpture frontality does not *have* to act as a guide to relevant attitudes toward
the art object. As long as sculpture involves itself with frontality as one of many aspects of an object and therefore as a physical condition of objects, frontality is tied to
the question of knowledge, knowledge for which any kind of information might be
relevant. Since most Cubist or Constructivist sculptors saw both painting and sculpture
as a branch of natural science and therefore tied to questions of knowledge about
things in the world, most of them gravitated toward a frontal arrangement of forms.
Boccioni's *Development of a Bottle in Space* is primarily frontal; most of Lipchitz's and
Laurens's still-life or figural compositions are frontal; and early Constructivism likewise
tended toward frontality. But their frontality was a way of presenting knowledge of the
object collected over time. It sought to collapse into one view intimations of, or
information about, all possible views. Their frontality refers simultaneously to the existence of the sculpture as an object (only one of whose multiple aspects the perceiver
sees at a given moment) and to the epistemological problem this poses. The statement

148
Cubi I.
(alternate view)

of this problem implies that any strategy one might have for solving it is relevant, as is any experience one might choose to have of the object.

Now, for Smith it became increasingly important to distinguish between the natural conditions of objects and the natural conditions of sculpture, which is to say that he felt compelled to exclude from the experience of sculpture itself the question of how we might know *any* object in the world. It is obvious that to do this he looked to frontality *as a convention,* for within a convention distinctions become possible, and through distinctions meaning also becomes possible.

The *Cubis* present a face to the viewer.[8] The very fact that one can speak of a face attests to the fact that they are freestanding objects. But unlike a neutral object like a cube, it is the only face they meaningfully have. The face itself expresses the disjunction between their condition as physical entities and their condition as sculpture.

In a sense Judd is right to see the *Cubis* as objects, as drawing that has become a monolithic possession of the third dimension. But he is wrong to think that they are thereby purged of a sense of illusion. The *Cubis* become "monoliths" in the sense that Sartre uses the term at the beginning of *What Is Literature?* when he demonstrates how a poet's treatment of words transforms them into objects. There he distinguishes between words in prose, which fade into the transparent instruments for communicating meaning, and words in a poem, which maintain a certain thickness or substance. To explain what he means, he quotes two lines from Mallarmé's "Brise marine":

Fuir! là-bas fuir! Je sens que des oiseaux sont ivres

. . . .

Mais, ô mon coeur, entends le chant des matelots!

---

[8] My license to speak of the sculpture in this way, rather than thinking of it as totally passive and determined by the *viewer's* motions, comes both from my sense of the sculpture and from Smith's own comments, like the one quoted in fn. 7.

[To flee! To flee there! I feel that birds are drunk

. . . .

But, oh, my heart, hear the song of the sailors!]

And then Sartre says, "This 'but' which rises like a monolith at the threshold of the sentence does not tie the second [line] to the preceding one. It colors it with a certain reserved nuance, with 'private associations' which penetrate it completely. In the same way, certain poems begin with 'and.' This conjunction no longer indicates to the mind an operation which is to be carried out; it extends throughout the paragraph to give it the absolute quality of a *sequel*. For the poet, the sentence has a tonality, a taste; by means of it he tastes for their own sake the irritating flavors of objection, of reserve, of disjunction. He carries them to the absolute. He makes them real properties of the sentence, which becomes an utter objection without being an objection *to* anything precise . . . the ensemble of the words chosen functions as an *image* of the interrogative or restrictive nuance."[9]

Sartre uses the word "monolith" with all of its connotative system intact. Like a dolmen, it stands at a fixed point in space, inert, immobile, and physically resistant. Like those signposts of neolithic culture, it also exists in an ideational space, a fulcrum on which natural phenomena are balanced against an abstract system of meaning. The monolith in this sense embodies the idea of relationship.

It is on this level, not on the level of style or attitude toward material, that Smith's *Cubis* are monolithic. At the focal point of our line of vision, Smith places a sculpture whose meaning, like Mallarmé's "but," reads as disjunctiveness itself, as the complete separation of modes of experience. To understand the image is to understand at the same time the palpable fact of the distance that separates the viewer from the object. That this meaning may be provoked by a glimpsed remnant of the human figure renders the absolute quality of disjunction no less abstract.

The *Cubis* allowed Smith to work at a scale approaching the one of his fantasy railway

[9] *What Is Literature?* (New York: Harper & Row, 1965), p. 11.

car from Voltri. Because their elements were fabricated by Smith and his assistant, the *Cubis* could be much larger than the *Voltri–Bolton Landing* pieces, which were limited by the size of the metal-working tools that were the basic units of their construction. The great scale of the *Cubis* is important to their visual meaning, since it makes even more disconcerting the way perception of the objects equivocates between flatness and bulk, between line and volume. There is an aggressive quality to the size of the *Cubis;* like the rest of Smith's work, they are not part of a vocabulary of form to be fondled or possessed. And this was also true of the colossal sculpture Smith dreamed of at Voltri, just as it was true that the sexual content of Smith's earliest work continued to possess his imagination: "I could have made a car with the nude bodies of machines, undressed of their detail and teeth. . . . In a year I could have made a train." The formal outcome of this set of feelings was a group of sculptures as yet unrivaled by any artist working in America.

Annotated Bibliography of Smith's Statements, Lectures, and Essays

With the exception of the first item, which refers to private papers, this bibliography lists in chronological order every public statement made by Smith, whether lecture, radio interview, or published article, and indicates the most accessible record of each. The references are annotated and cross-referenced ("Smith," followed by the entry number), so that the reader may see how often Smith's statements came from a small repertoire of ideas that he used to define his public image. For the relevant secondary material on the artist, the reader is directed to the footnotes in the text.

1. The Archives of American Art, Detroit, Michigan.
Eight reels of microfilm: I–V contain drafts for speeches, letters, sketchbooks, and notebooks by Smith; VI records the scrapbook kept by Marion Willard, Smith's dealer from 1938 to 1956, of exhibitions, reviews, and articles; VII and VIII reproduce the photographic record made by Ugo Mulas of nearly everything in the estate at the time of Smith's death. Access to this material is granted by permission of the executors of Smith's estate.

2. David Smith by David Smith. Edited by Cleve Gray. New York: Holt, Rinehart & Winston, 1969. Besides excerpts (unannotated and confusingly interwoven) from many of the articles and speeches listed here, this book contains some previously unpublished material of scholarly interest. Valuable information about Smith's early life and career is contained in the autobiographical notes, probably written in the early fifties (pp. 24–33), to which Dorothy Dehner, Smith's first wife, has added commentary by means of footnotes (p. 174), and a statement headed "Atmosphere of early '30s" from a 1952 sketchbook (p. 35). For insight into the later work, the Voltri notes written by Smith in June 1962 are useful (pp. 42–45, 156).

3. "Abstract Art in America." Speech given at the United American Artists Forum, New York, February 1940. Archive IV/332, 851. Excerpted in The New York Artist 1 (April 1940): 5–6, and David Smith by David Smith, p. 132.
Smith's argument for abstraction is reminiscent of the kind of reasoning used by Hans Hofmann in his description of "the higher aesthetic third" (see Search for the Real [Andover, Mass: Addison Gallery of American Art, 1948], p. 47). This is the first time that Smith speaks of the commonality of sculpture and painting, "the only difference being the material use of a dimension—in place of an indicated one."

4. [Remarks made in interview] in Ernest Watson, "David Smith." American Artist 4 (March 1940): 20–22.
Valuable for early opinion on abstraction and for biographical information.

5. "Abstract Art." The New York Artist 1 (April 1940): 5–6.
Excerpts from the speech given to the United American Artists Forum, February 1940; see Smith 3.

6. "Sculpture." *Architectural Record* 88 (October 1940): 77-80.
Smith discusses the properties and potentials of different metals available to the welder-sculptor, as well as the application of color and the use of movement. His attitude toward architecture is, at this point, benign; he feels that sculptors and architects can collaborate usefully and that they both value similar formal ideas. This attitude was to change in the fifties; see Smith 43, 45, 52.

7. [Commentary] in *Medals for Dishonor*. Marion Willard Gallery, New York, November 1940.

8. [Speech] at Skidmore College, Saratoga Springs, New York, February 17, 1947. Archive IV/744. Excerpted in *David Smith by David Smith*, p. 133.
Much of this is taken directly from the February 1940 speech, Smith 3. What is new is the idea that "art can be a communication between one unconscious and the other," and references to Ernst Kris's remarks about the narcissistic investment of the artist in his work.

9. "The Sculptor's Relationship to Museum, Dealer, and Public." Speech given at the First Woodstock Conference of Artists, Woodstock, New York, August 29, 1947. Archive IV/910. Excerpted in *David Smith by David Smith*, p. 137.

10. "The Landscape"; "Spectres Are"; "Sculpture Is." Marion Willard Gallery, New York, April 1947. Archive I/500. Excerpted in *Possibilities* 1 (Winter 1947-1948): 25, and *David Smith by David Smith*, p. 155.

11. "I Have Never Looked at a Landscape"; "Sculpture Is." *Possibilities* 1 (Winter 1947-1948): 25. See Smith 10.

12. "The Golden Eagle—a Recital." *Tiger's Eye* 1 (June 1948): 81-82.

13. [Statement] at *Herald Tribune* Forum, New York, held in conjunction with the New York City Board of Education, March 19, 1950. Archive IV/332. Reprinted in *David Smith by David Smith*, p. 132.
This was the first appearance of a theme that was never to leave Smith's public pronouncements—the idea that a man's art springs directly from his life and the particularities of his historical moment. Therefore, Smith argues, contemporary art cannot be understood through an aesthetic developed from past styles.

14. "The Teaching of Sculpture." Speech given at the Midwestern College Art Conference, University of Kentucky, Louisville, Kentucky, October 27, 1950. Archive IV/336-345.
Another of Smith's repeated themes was that the words used by art historians and critics were damaging to the artist because they limited his possibilities within the boundaries of an already-conceived definition. Smith also advised the students to read Boas, psychoanalytic material, and James Joyce.

15. [Lecture] at American University, Washington, D.C., January 9, 1951. Archive I/1058.
Although differently worded, this repeats many of the ideas in the 1940 "Abstract Art in America" speech, Smith 3.

16. [Captions] in *David Smith*. Marion Willard Gallery, New York, March-April 1951.
Archive III/13-16. Reprinted in *David Smith by David Smith*, pp. 72-73.

17. [Speech] at Bennington College, Bennington, Vermont, November 11, 1951. Archive IV/346-350. This was published as "The Language Is

Image," *Arts and Architecture* 69 (February 1952): 20–21, reprinted in *David Smith* (Cambridge, Mass.: Fogg Museum, 1966), and excerpted in *David Smith by David Smith*, p. 71.
Once again, Smith rejects stylistic labels and closed definitions. He speaks of the associations that cluster around any single image. As an example he recounts the creation of *Hudson River Landscape.*

18. [Speech] at Williams College, Williamstown, Massachusetts, December 17, 1951. A rerun of the Bennington College speech, Smith 17.

19. [Notes] for Elaine de Kooning, 1951. Archive IV/490–501. Reprinted in "Notes for David Smith Makes a Sculpture," *Art News* 68 (January 1969): 35–38. Excerpted in *David Smith by David Smith*, pp. 22, 50, 55, 68.
These notes were written for Elaine de Kooning for her article, "David Smith Makes a Sculpture," *Art News* 50 (September 1951): 38–41. Smith discusses his working procedures for the most part. He mentions the role of drawing in his work and the cost of his materials. He also writes: "I do not accept the monolithic limit in the tradition of sculpture. Sculpture is as free as the mind, as complex as life. . . ."

20. "Problems of the Contemporary Sculptor." Speech given at the Metropolitan Art Association meeting, Detroit, Michigan, January 20, 1952. Archive IV/351–356. Excerpted in *David Smith by David Smith*, p. 137.
A reworking of the ideas in the Bennington speech, Smith 17; the *Hudson River Landscape* example is used verbatim.

21. "The New Sculpture." Speech given at a symposium by that name at the Museum of Modern Art, New York, February 21, 1952. Ar-

chive IV/357–362. Excerpted in *David Smith by David Smith*, pp. 17, 20, 50, 59, 77.
The major new idea in this speech is a statement about iron as a material. Smith says that his commitment to it comes in part from its lack of associations with previously known "high art," and in part from its symbolic references to the dawn of culture, to industrial power, and to destruction. He also develops the phrasing for the admonition he was to repeat often: that his sculpture is his identity; that it comes from his "work stream"; and that he will accept no one's judgment of it.

22. "The Language Is Image." *Arts and Architecture* 69 (February 1952): 20–21. Publication of the Bennington speech, November 1951, Smith 17. Reprinted in the *Bennington College Alumnae Quarterly 3* (November 1952).

23. "The Modern Sculptor and His Material." Speech given at the University of Michigan, Ann Arbor, Michigan, April 18, 1952. Archive IV/480–482.
This is mainly a reworking of the Bennington College speech, November 1951, Smith 17.

24. [Speech] given at the Walker Art Center, Minneapolis, Minnesota, April 24, 1952. Published in *Everyday Art Quarterly*, no. 23 (Winter 1952), pp. 16–21. Excerpted in *David Smith by David Smith*, pp. 52, 164; reprinted in *David Smith* (Cambridge, Mass.: Fogg Museum, 1966).
This is a composite of the Detroit (January 1952), Museum of Modern Art (February 1952), and Ann Arbor (April 1952) speeches, Smith 20, 21, 23.

25. "The Sculptor and His Problems." Speech given at the Woodstock Conference of Artists, Woodstock, New York, August 23, 1952. Archive

IV/371-383. Excerpted in *David Smith by David Smith*, pp. 117, 139.
Smith again speaks of the need of the artist to reject the set definitions of style formulated by historians and critics. He calls on the artist to act with "belligerent vitality." He repeats the idea that visual responses to objects are not confined within specific limits but overlay the image with unexpected and uncontrollable associations.

26. [Speech] on WNYC-New York, December 30, 1952. Archive IV/362-366. Excerpted in *The Museum and Its Friends—18 Living American Artists* (Whitney Museum of American Art, New York, March 5-April 12, 1969), pp. 36-37, and in *David Smith by David Smith*, pp. 57, 60, 71.
This is largely a reworking of the 1952 Woodstock speech.

27. "Who Is the Artist? How Does He Act?" *Everyday Art Quarterly*, no. 23 (Winter 1952), pp. 16-21. Reprinted in *Numero* 1, no. 3 (May-June 1953): 21. Excerpted in *Art in America* 53 (August-September 1965): 122, and in *Contemporary American Paintings and Sculpture* (Urbana: University of Illinois, 1953), pp. 223-224. Publication of the Walker Art Center speech, April 1952, Smith 24.

28. [Speech] at the Portland Museum of Art, Portland, Oregon, March 23, 1952. Archive IV/384-390. Excerpted in *David Smith by David Smith*, pp. 54, 68, 104.
Smith refers to his metamorphosis from painter to sculptor and to his contact with the Picasso-Gonzalez constructions. He adds, "Cubism brought about a form concept which produced a total liberation in viewing and at the same time made the concept in painting and sculp-

ture one." He speaks of his need to draw. He then repeats the formula about the sculpture as his identity and its relation to his "work stream", the symbolism of steel (see Smith 21); and finally his rejection of the monolithic ideal, which he calls "the Galatea complex which made the sculptor the conceptual slave of material. . . ."

29. [Speech] given at the University of Arkansas, Fayetteville, Arkansas, April 22, 1952. Archive IV/406-409. Published as "Thoughts on Sculpture," *College Art Journal* 13 (Winter 1954): 97-100; reprinted in *David Smith* (Cambridge, Mass.: Fogg Museum, 1966).
This is a reworking of the Bennington speech, November 1951, Smith 17.

30. "A Sculptor's Point of View." Speech given at the Southwestern Art Conference, University of Oklahoma, Norman, Oklahoma, May 1, 1953. Archive IV/412-416. Published as "Second Thoughts on Sculpture," *College Art Journal* 13 (Spring 1954): 203-207.
In part this is a repeat of the Museum of Modern Art speech, Smith 21. Smith argues here that sculpture comes from a deep need in man, formed early in his individual history and in his collective, cultural history. He repeats the idea that the artist's only relevant relationship is to the present historical moment (what Smith persisted in terming the artist's "filial epoch"); repeats the argument against a monolithic definition of sculpture; calls for "belligerent vitality"; and speaks of the salutary effect of art's embracing those aspects of culture that had always been considered "vulgar."

31. [Statement] in *12 Peintres et Sculpteurs Américains Contemporains*. Musée National

d'Art Moderne, Paris, April–June, 1953.
Excerpted from the Museum of Modern Art
speech, February 1952, Smith 21.

32. "Economic Support of Art in America Today." Speech given at the American Federa-
tion of Artists Conference, Corning, New York,
October 30, 1953. Archive IV/422–427. Excerpted
in *David Smith by David Smith*, pp. 166, 169.
Again a plea for the artist to find his own identity and to make his art from that.

33. [Statement] in "Art and Religion: Symposium." *Art Digest* 28 (December 15, 1953): 11.

34. "Thoughts on Sculpture." *College Art Journal* 13 (Winter 1954): 97. Publication of Arkansas
speech, April 1953, Smith 29.

35. "The Artist's Image." Speech given at the
College Art Association Conference, Philadel-
phia, Pennsylvania, January 30, 1954. Archive
IV/428–431. Excerpted in *David Smith by David
Smith*, p. 74.
This is taken in part from the Bennington speech,
November 1951, Smith 17.

36. "Second Thoughts on Sculpture." *College
Art Journal* 13 (Spring 1954): 203–207. Publication
of Norman, Oklahoma, speech, May 1953, Smith
30.

37. "The Artist, the Critics, and the Scholar."
Speech given at the Albright Art Gallery, Buffalo, New York, April 23, 1954. Archive IV/432–
436. Excerpted in *David Smith by David Smith*,
p. 166.
This is largely a reworking of the Corning, New
York, speech, October 1953, Smith 32.

38. "Tradition." Speech given at Columbia University, New York, June 18, 1954. Archive IV/437–
440.

Taken from the Philadelphia speech, January
1954, Smith 35.

39. "The Attitudes toward Tradition of the
Contemporary Artist." Speech given at the
Woodstock Conference of Artists, Woodstock,
New York, August 6, 1954. Archive IV/441–443.
Excerpted in *David Smith by David Smith*, pp.
134, 162.
The statement "Tradition comes wrapped in
word pictures" is the argument against pre-
established definitions about what art should be.
Smith repeats the demand that art should be
the artist's identity.

40. "What Makes a Student Good?" Speech
given at the Midwestern Art Conference, Indiana University, Bloomington, Indiana, April
1954.

41. "Drawing." Speech given at Sophie New-
comb College, New Orleans, Louisiana, March
21, 1955. Archive IV/451–453. Excerpted in *David
Smith by David Smith*, pp. 84, 86, 88.

42. "Gonzalez: First Master of the Torch." *Art
News* 54 (February 1956): 34–37.
In researching this article, Smith wrote to Roberta
Gonzalez asking questions about her father
(IV/770) but apparently received no reply. He
did however ask for and receive information
from Henri Goetz, who had been a friend of
Gonzalez's (Archive V/771–772).

43. "Sculpture and Architecture." *Arts* 31 (May
1957): 20. This was later given as a speech at
Pratt Institute, New York, November 7, 1963,
Smith 56.
Smith voices his resentment against architects
for not understanding and for misusing sculpture.

44. [Letter to the editor] in *Arts* 31 (June 1957): 7.
A public denial of the authenticity of statements ascribed to him by Seldon Rodman in *Conversations with Artists* (New York: Devin-Adair, 1957), pp. 126–130.

45. "Alcoa Foundation Lecture." Rensselaer Polytechnic Institute, Troy, New York, November 1957. Archive IV/454–459. Excerpted in *David Smith by David Smith*, p. 58.
Smith refers to the Bauhaus idea of collaboration between artists and architects. He says that this partnership is impossible and refers to the arrogance of the architect.

46. [Statement] in "Is Today's Artist with or against the Past?" *Art News* 57 (September 1958): 38.
Smith speaks of his affinity for non-Western and preclassical art. He mentions his grandmother's Bible "with reproductions of Egyptian and Sumerian art in it."

47. [Statement about *The Hero*, 1952] in "Two Recent Purchases." *Brooklyn Museum Bulletin* 19 (September 1958): 11–13.

48. [Speech] given at Ohio State University, Athens, Ohio, April 17, 1959. Archive IV/460–462. Excerpted in *David Smith by David Smith*, pp. 34, 56, 137, 164.
Smith refers to his adolescent days in Ohio and how as a young art student he thought that sculpture could be made only by someone initiated into the use of sanctified materials like marble and bronze. Now, he says, he realizes that no aesthetic lines are drawn. He then repeats the caution against accepting set definitions. He adds that he doesn't know when he starts it how a sculpture will end but that the process is part of his search for identity.

49. "Notes on My Work." *Arts* 34 (February 1960): 44.
A statement about his beginnings as a sculptor. Reprinted in *David Smith* (Cambridge, Mass.: Fogg Museum, 1966).

50. "Memories to Myself." Speech given at the 18th Conference of the National Committee on Art Education at the Museum of Modern Art, May 5, 1960. Reprinted in *Journal of the Archives of American Art* 8 (April 1968): 11–16. Excerpted in *David Smith by David Smith*, pp. 58, 75, 77, 130, 139.
Smith speaks of his resentment of the way art is taught in schools and of the prejudices of history. He explains why it is so difficult to teach art students what is really important.

51. [Letter to the editor] *Arts* 34 (June 1960): 5, and *Art News* 59 (Summer 1960): 5.
Smith renounces his sculpture *17 h's* because it has been painted without his permission.

52. "Self-Portrait of an American Sculptor." Interview on the BBC, June 16, 1961. Tape is in Archive.
Smith speaks of his dislike for modern architecture; of the importance of his trip to Europe in the thirties.

53. [Statement] in *The Whitney Review*. New York: Whitney Museum of American Art, 1962, n.p.

54. "David Smith." Interview with Katherine Kuh in *The Artist's Voice: Talks with Seventeen Artists*. New York: Harper & Row, 1962, pp. 219–234. Reprinted in *David Smith* (Cambridge, Mass.: Fogg Museum, 1966).

55. [Letter] in Giovanni Carandente, *Voltron.* Philadelphia: University of Pennsylvania Press, 1964, pp. 11–15.
Letter discussing the Voltri commission, written to English art critic David Sylvester in November 1962.

56. "Modern Sculpture and Society." Speech given at Pratt Institute, New York, November 7, 1963. Archive IV/690–691. Excerpted in *David Smith by David Smith*, pp. 60, 134, 135.
This is identical to the article published in *Arts* in 1957, Smith 43.

57. "David Smith Interviewed by David Sylvester." *Living Arts* 1 (April 1964): 4–13.

58. "The Secret Letter." Interview with Thomas Hess in *David Smith*, Marlborough-Gerson Gallery, New York, October 1964. Excerpted in *David Smith by David Smith*, pp. 114, 118, 123, 172.
Smith discusses his relation to advanced art, his use of color, the burnishing on the *Cubis*, his childhood.

59. "Profiles." Interview with Marian Honesko on WNCN–New York, October 25, 1964. Tape in Archive.
Smith speaks about not wanting to appeal to touch.

60. "David Smith: Welding Master of Bolton Landing." Interview with Frank O'Hara on WNDT-TV, New York, November 11, 1964. Excerpted in *Art in America* 54 (January–February 1966): 47, and in *David Smith by David Smith*, pp. 124, 187.

61. [Slide talk] given at Bennington College, Bennington, Vermont, May 12, 1965. Published as "Some Late Words from David Smith," ed. Gene Baro, *Art International* 9 (October 1965): 47–51. Excerpted in *David Smith by David Smith*, pp. 118, 125.
Smith discusses individual works from the late fifties and sixties.

62. "Some Late Words from David Smith." Edited by Gene Baro. *Art International* 9 (October 1965): 47–51.
See Smith 61.

Index

Italicized
page numbers
refer to
illustrations.